Amanda Keddie • Michael Flood

Young Men's Online Lives

Cultivating Critical Digital Dispositions for Gender Justice

palgrave
macmillan

Amanda Keddie
Faculty of Arts and Education
Deakin University
Melbourne, VIC, Australia

Michael Flood
School of Justice
Queensland University of Technology
Brisbane, QLD, Australia

ISBN 978-3-031-99979-6 ISBN 978-3-031-99980-2 (eBook)
https://doi.org/10.1007/978-3-031-99980-2

This Palgrave Macmillan imprint is published by the registered company Springer Nature Switzerland AG.
The registered company address is: Gewerbestrasse 11, 6330 Cham, Switzerland

If disposing of this product, please recycle the paper.

Acknowledgements

The research reported in this book was supported by the Australian Government through the eSafety Commissioner. The views expressed herein are those of the authors and are not necessarily those of the Australian Government. We would like to acknowledge Joshua Roose who, with Amanda Keddie and Michael Flood, was part of the research team and David Cao and Mark Yin who were the youth researchers on the project.

The use of the Generative AI tools, Elicit and Chat GPT was drawn on to support some of the writing and editing for this book. Elicit was used to find and summarise the findings of relevant academic research in each chapter of the book to enable a broad range of literature to be cited. Chat GPT was used to generate summaries of relevant reports to be integrated into the writing and to generate the activities in Chap. 6 (more details about how the activities were generated are included in Chap. 6). Chat GPT was also used to create the index. All AI-generated outputs were critically reviewed and checked for accuracy.

Competing Interests The authors have no competing interests to declare that are relevant to the content of this manuscript.

Ethics Approval The research presented in this book received ethical clearance from Deakin University. Participants under 18 received permission to participate in the study from their parents/guardians.

About This Book

In Australia and globally recent media and public discourse has expressed strong concerns about the gender-based harms arising from young men's online behaviours—from revenge porn and the circulation of AI deepfake pornography to anxieties about schoolboys being radicalised into misogyny through their engagement with the manosphere. These concerns have prompted renewed scrutiny on boys and masculinity and produced a sense of urgency around addressing these online harms. They have provided a strong warrant for research that seeks to better understand how young men are navigating their online worlds. This book presents findings from a qualitative study of 117 young men in Australia. The book provides comprehensive and in-depth insights into the factors that influence, motivate and inform young men's online experiences. In foregrounding a diversity of young men's voices, the book responds to calls for more nuance and care in how we debate the gendered impact of social media on young men's lives. As such we draw attention to the tensions and complexities in how young men navigate negative and positive online experiences, including their critical engagement with harmful online content. Against this backdrop, the book presents a case for fostering young men's critical digital dispositions towards more gender just engagements online. It provides a conceptual framework and series of activity ideas for fostering these dispositions through curatorial intentionality, scepticism, ethical engagement and reflexivity (Pangrazio, 2018). Towards gender justice, this framework seeks to support young men to critically engage with and transform gendered digital harms.

Young Men's Online Lives

Contents

About the Authors

Amanda Keddie is Professor of Education at Deakin University. Her research examines the processes, practices and conditions that can impact on the pursuit of social justice in education settings. Amanda's qualitative research has been based within the Australian, English and American schooling contexts and is focused on addressing gender-based violence through educative approaches. She is internationally recognised in this field. Amanda is the author of *Supporting and Educating Young Muslim Women: Stories from Australia and the UK* (2017), *Educating for Diversity and Social Justice* (2012) and *The Affective Intensities of Masculinity in Shaping Gendered Experience: From Little Boys, Big Boys Grow* (2022). She is the co-author of *Teaching Boys: Developing Classroom Practices That Work* (2007).

Michael Flood is an internationally recognised researcher on men, masculinities and gender; violence against women; and violence prevention. He has made significant contributions to scholarly and public understanding of men's involvements in preventing violence against women and building gender equality, and to scholarship and programming regarding violence and violence prevention and men and masculinities. Michael is the author of *Engaging Men and Boys in Violence Prevention* (2019), the co-author of *Masculinity and Violent Extremism* (2022), and the lead editor of *Engaging Men in Building Gender Equality* (2015) and *The International Encyclopedia of Men and Masculinities* (2007). He is also an advocate and educator.

CHAPTER 1

Introduction

Abstract This chapter provides a context for understanding the gender harms associated with young men's online engagements. It canvases key contemporary debates about these harms that have led to renewed scrutiny on boys, men and masculinity and produced a sense of urgency around addressing what seems to have become a ubiquitous term in discussions of young men's online behaviours, 'toxic' masculinity. The chapter situates this scrutiny and urgency within a broader context of volatile and polarising gender politics where there exists simultaneously, a strong focus on redressing misogyny, sexism and other forms of gender-based violence and a strong backlash that cast men and boys as the real victims of gender discrimination. Amid these politics, the chapter argues for the significance of research that better understands the nuances and complexities of young men's online worlds, the imperative of listening to their voices, and the importance of recognising the criticality and agency of their online engagements. The chapter explores young men's positive and negative engagements online and describes the qualitative study upon which the book is based. It concludes with an overview of each of the subsequent chapters.

Keywords Young men • Gender harms • Online engagements • Contemporary debates • Volatile gender politics

A. Keddie, M. Flood, *Young Men's Online Lives*,
https://doi.org/10.1007/978-3-031-99980-2_1

Contemporary Debates: Young Men's Online Lives

Recent media and public discourse in Australia and globally is replete with concerns about young men's online behaviours, from schoolboys circulating AI deepfake pornography of their female classmates and teachers (Hunt & Higgins, 2024), revenge porn and the sending of unsolicited 'dick picks' (Ringrose et al., 2021) to anxieties about the manosphere radicalising young men into misogyny (Bates, 2021; Ging, 2019). A Plan International survey in mid-2020 described social media as 'the new frontier for gendered violence', finding that 65% of 1000 Australian teenagers and young women had been exposed to a spectrum of online violence with half reporting emotional and mental distress (Plan International, 2020). These concerns and findings have led to renewed scrutiny on boys and masculinity and produced a sense of urgency around addressing what seems to have become a ubiquitous term in discussions of young men's online behaviours, 'toxic' masculinity. Toxic masculinity (a highly contentious term) refers to cultural norms and behaviours associated with traditional ideas of masculinity that can be harmful. It includes traits like suppressing emotions, valuing dominance and aggression over empathy, and discouraging vulnerability or seeking help. These norms can lead to negative outcomes such as emotional repression, unhealthy relationships, and perpetuating sexism or violence.

Recent research in Australia and the UK has examined the rise and influence of harmful social media figures such as Andrew Tate (an American-British personality known for promoting misogynistic, sexist, and homophobic content that exemplifies 'toxic' masculinity) (Wescott et al., 2023; Haslop et al., 2024; Roberts et al., 2025). This research highlights how so-called 'manfluencers' like Tate, who enjoy significant popularity among boys and young men (Haslop et al., 2024), work to defend and normalise patriarchal inequalities (Roberts et al., 2025). Their influence is seen as contributing to a resurgence of sexism in schools, legitimising a regressive form of male supremacy that has particularly harmful effects on female teachers and schoolgirls (Wescott et al., 2023). There are fears that the increasingly popular online 'manosphere' and especially groups such as the incels (Involuntary Celibates) are radicalising young men into misogyny (Bates, 2021; Botto & Gottzén, 2023). Incels are online communities primarily consisting of young men who express anger and frustration towards women for rejecting them romantically or sexually and who often engage in discussions where they fantasise about violence against women. Such fears have led to a proliferation of funding and programs to tackle harmful messages of 'toxic' masculinity on social media, education initiatives for school-age boys that seek to counteract dangerous gender stereotypes, and public awareness campaigns and community action focused on promoting 'healthy masculinities' (Keddie et al., 2022).

Concerns about boys, men and 'harmful' masculinities are far from new with research in this space spanning decades and disciplines. What seems to be new in this space is how these concerns are playing out in the post #MeToo climate of volatile and polarising gender politics. In this climate there simultaneously exists strong public and media support for action to address sexism and gender-based violence but also powerful backlash discourses where men and boys are cast as the real victims of gender discrimination—unfairly blamed and shamed for sexism and gender-based violence. Also new in this space is the strong public and political support for banning social media in Australia for young people under the age of 16 (to come into effect by the end of 2025). The legislation put forth by the Australian Federal Government in late 2024 aims to prohibit young people's access to social media platforms, including TikTok, Instagram, Twitter (X) Snapchat, Facebook and YouTube. Such prohibition responds to increasing concerns about how social media is negatively impacting on the mental health of young people especially in relation to increased rates of anxiety and depression (Kaye & Menon, 2024). As reported by the Australian Psychological Society, the mental health distress of young people can be connected to the use of social media (APS, 2024).

All of this provides a strong warrant for research that seeks to better understand how young men are navigating their online worlds where they spend much of their time (on average around 15 hours per week, eSafety Commissioner, 2021). At present policy and practice-based initiatives in this area are not informed by targeted research about how young men are navigating their sense of identity, purpose, belonging and acceptance online.

Young men's voices have not been foregrounded in these debates over online spaces and social media. While concerns abound about the harms young men are perpetuating online, we do not have a comprehensive understanding of the online experiences of young men from their perspectives. What also tends to be absent from these debates are accounts of young men's positive engagements in online spaces. Social media platforms are providing young men with positive opportunities for identity exploration, relationship building, and prosocial behaviours (Wang &

Edwards, 2016). Online communities can be highly supportive spaces of belonging, and positive for physical and mental health (Robinson & Robertson, 2010; Ellis et al., 2014).

Young men's online experiences are the focus of this book. The book presents findings from an Australian qualitative study of 117 young men (aged 16–21) from diverse backgrounds. These young men took part in a series of two-hour focus groups, engaging in open-ended discussion of their online experiences. The research was funded by the eSafety Commission (Australia) (eSafety Commissioner, 2024). Through a youth-centred, strengths-based approach, the research provides comprehensive and in-depth insights into the factors that influence, motivate, and inform young men's online experiences. In platforming a diversity of young men's voices, the book responds to calls for more 'nuance and care' in how we debate the gendered impact of social media on young men's lives:

> Rather than framing social media as a risk in general, it is helpful to focus on the dangers, but also the positive potential, of particular kinds of use in a specific context. This requires understanding how specific patterns of social media use reflect and interact with other offline factors. (Koester & Marcus, 2024, p. 8)

This book provides this nuance and care by highlighting the tensions and complexities of young men's online engagements. While we recognise the potential harms of these engagements, we also draw attention to young men's positive engagements and experiences including their critical engagement with harmful online content. Such insights are imperative in better supporting young men to navigate online spaces in ways that minimise harm for themselves and others (Ging & Siapera, 2018; Koester & Marcus, 2024). The following provides a brief overview of research relating to young men's positive and negative engagements online with a particular focus on gender and social media.

Young Men's Positive and Negative Engagements Online

As with young people more broadly, young men engage with a diversity of online platforms, with different platforms providing different opportunities for self-expression and social interaction. For this demographic, the use of social media platforms such as TikTok, Instagram, Facebook, X (formerly Twitter) and Snapchat is central for social connection, maintaining relationships and forming new communities around shared interests (Wang & Edwards, 2016; Wright & Li, 2011).

These social media platforms provide a context where young men can express and experiment with different aspects of their identity and showcase their talents, creativity, and personal style through posts, photos, videos, and other forms of content creation (Koester & Marcus, 2024). They also provide a context where young men can explore their masculinities through visual self-presentations on social networking sites (Siibak, 2010), engaging with online self-improvement content, such as 'fitspiration' (Palmér, 2015) and discussing health issues (Tyler & Williams, 2014) including relating to mental health (Ellis et al., 2014) and anxiety (Drioli-Phillips et al., 2021). Many young men find these spaces useful for gaining advice about their insecurities relating to issues of masculinity and identity (Maloney et al., 2022). For LGBTIQ+ youth, social media and other online spaces are an invaluable means of connecting with others in their community and fostering a sense of belonging and self-acceptance (Byron et al., 2019; Thomas et al., 2007).

Also central to fostering young men's connections with others are gaming platforms. Gaming has become a significant part of youth culture, with young men often spending substantial amounts of time engaging in online gaming activities (Wack & Tantleff-Dunn, 2009). Gaming communities generated through platforms such as Xbox Live, Steam, PlayStation Network and Twitch enable social connection through architectures that support multiplayer interaction. Such architectures create opportunities for socialisation and teamwork. They can generate a sense of belonging and camaraderie (Weinstein & James, 2022).

While social media and gaming platforms clearly provide young men with positive online experiences, especially in relation to social connection and belonging, they are also spaces that can proliferate harm. Gender-based harms are common within male-dominated online spaces such as gaming, pornography and sexting. These spaces can be breeding grounds for misogyny, harassment, and disrespectful behaviour towards women and girls (Ringrose et al., 2021). Boys and young men may be exposed to harmful ideologies that promote the objectification, belittlement, or degradation of women. Online gaming, for example, is rife with hypermasculine and heteronormative content (Liu, 2022). The Geena Davis Institute's (2021) analysis of gender representations in the content of the top 20 Twitch streamers found that male characters outnumbered female characters, male characters were much more likely to be leaders (over 75% of the time) and female characters were likely to be sexualised (Geena Davis Institute, 2021). Such gendered content can reinforce and perpetuate harmful attitudes and behaviours (Ging, 2019; Baker et al., 2024).

Sexting (the exchange of sexually explicit messages, images, or videos) is another avenue where gendered harms proliferate. Although sexting can involve consenting and mutual exchanges that foster sexual and relational intimacy, it can also be highly problematic when it involves a lack of consent, threats to privacy, and the objectification of bodies (Flood, 2024; eSafety Commission, 2023). Sexting in the form of the non-consensual distribution of intimate images is particularly harmful and well recognised as causing emotional distress and damage to personal and social reputations (Dekker et al., 2019). Sexting also promotes distorted perceptions of relationships and intimacy. In a study that examined issues of risk relating to sexting practices with young men, for example, Ravn et al. (2019) highlighted the use of derogatory labels such as 'slut' and 'creep' to police and reinforce gendered norms. While the label 'slut' was employed to stigmatise and shame overly sexual women (i.e., those that willingly shared sexualised images), the label 'creep' was used for men who sent unsolicited explicit images (often referred to as 'dick pics'). Both labels denote a violation of social boundaries—portraying women as deviating from traditional expectations of modesty, and men as socially awkward or predatory. The application of these labels reflects and perpetuates well recognised gendered power dynamics, where women's sexual agency is policed through shaming and men's inappropriate behaviours are acknowledged but often normalised (Ravn et al., 2019).

Young men's ease of access to online pornography is another significant challenge (eSafety Commission, 2023). As with sexting, exposure to explicit sexual content at a young age can shape boys' and young men's perceptions of consent, relationships, and bodies. Pornography often portrays unrealistic and harmful representations of sex, objectifying women and promoting aggressive and degrading behaviours. This can lead to distorted ideas about consent, intimacy and sex in ways that valorise dominance, control, and sexual prowess as central to notions of manhood (Flood, 2024; eSafety Commission, 2023).

Such distortions predominate in the manosphere—which is 'a broad collection of websites, forums, and other online spaces characterized by their misogynistic and anti-feminist content, which swoops in with clear messages to help men make sense of a changing world, particularly around gender and gender roles' (Equimundo, 2024). Young men tend to be directed to these sites through algorithms associated with male-identified accounts (Baker et al., 2024) or they may be enticed by the manosphere's simplistic narrative to explain their frustrations and insecurities and the sense of belonging this movement provides (Brito et al., 2024). There are concerns that these spaces are radicalising young men into misogyny (Bates, 2021; Baker et al., 2024):

> While misogyny predates the digital era, researchers point to the role of digital technologies in facilitating new and more virulent strains of hatred and violence directed at women … the mass circulation of anti-women and anti-feminist sentiments through online connectivity and scalability is unprecedented. (Brito et al., 2024, p. 11)

These positive and negative engagements are explored in this book. At the heart of this study lies a profound acknowledgment of the struggles faced by young men in comprehending their place in the world, both offline and online.

Amid broader contentious gender politics that tend to position young men as uncaring and uncritical of the digital content they consume, create and share, this book sheds light on the criticality and agency of young men's online engagement. It is imperative to recognise young men as critical consumers of online content rather than passive recipients. While young men do experience and perpetuate personal and relational harms online, they also demonstrate capacity and resources for minimising and preventing harms. In navigating the digital landscape, for example, many young men are critically aware of the algorithms shaping their online experiences, with a prevailing scepticism about algorithms potentially steering them toward harmful content and amplifying negative ideologies (Pangrazio, 2018; Santos-Meneses, 2021). They are also critically aware of the proliferation of misinformation in the content they consume and active in how they take up or reject this information (Koester & Marcus, 2024). By capturing the voices and experiences of young men, this book aspires to contribute to more comprehensive and nuanced understandings of young men's online lives.

The Research Context and Processes

The qualitative research that underpins this book was funded by the eSafety Commission, Australia's independent regulator for online safety. Led by researchers from Deakin University and the Queensland University of Technology, the study sought to explore the influences and motivations shaping young men's online experiences (eSafety Commissioner, 2024). Some of this research is published in the report *Being a young man online: Tensions, complexities and possibilities* (eSafety Commissioner, 2024). The study involved 117 young men aged between 16–21, 25 online focus groups and 25 follow up individual interviews. This group of participants was recruited to reflect the diverse range of backgrounds, identities and lived experiences of young men in Australia today.

Participants and Recruitment

All of the participants identified as men and were fluent in English. Fourteen identified as having a disability. A little over half of the participant cohort identified as Anglo-Australian. Forty-nine were from culturally and linguistically diverse (CALD) backgrounds, and four identified as First Nations. Further demographic details of the sample are given in Table 1.1.

All of the young men were allocated pseudonyms and a nomenclature to denote specific demographic factors in brackets, using the following:

- Age = number, e.g., 19
- Sexuality = S for Straight; G for Gay; B for Bisexual; Ax for Asexual; Q for Queer; U for Unsure/Questioning

Table 1.1 Demographic details of participants

Age	*%*	*Sexual identity*	*%*	*Employment*	*%*
16	18	Straight	76	Students	79
17	10	Gay	8	Working part- or full-time	17
18	19	Bisexual	9	Self-employed	1
19	19	Queer	2	Unemployed	3
20	19	Asexual	1		
21	15	Unsure/questioning	2		
		Prefer not to say	2		

- Culturally and Linguistically Diverse Background = CALD
- First Nations Status = First Nations
- Disability Status = D for Disability

For example, if a quote is attributed to "Jaden (19, G, CALD)", this tells the reader that Jaden is 19, identifies as gay, and is from a culturally and linguistically diverse or CALD background. The text "Alastair (16, B, D)" tells us that Alastair is 16, identifies as bisexual and has a disability, and the text "Bailey (16, S, CALD)" tells us that Bailey is 16, straight/heterosexual, and from a CALD background.

The research received ethical clearance from Deakin University. Participants under 18 received permission to participate in the study from their parents or guardians.

Methods

The study involved 25 online focus groups with four or five young men in each. To ensure that the questions, interview style and language for the interviews were as relevant to the young men as possible, the research team recruited and consulted four youth researchers from the Centre for Multicultural Youth (Victoria, Australia). These youth researchers participated in an initial in-person workshop with the research team where we discussed the research questions and developed a set of sub-questions and prompts reflecting the key research questions. We were mindful here of ensuring that the language for the questions was youth friendly. Two of the male youth researchers went on to carry out all of the focus group interviews. The research team worked with the youth researchers prior to and throughout the data collection period to ensure that there was consistency in how the interview schedule was approached and to debrief on the interview process including keeping to time, keeping on track, developing rapport and maintaining engagement.

The focus group interviews typically took around two hours. Participants were grouped according to age: the young men aged 16–18 were grouped together while the young men aged 19–21 were grouped together. The first section of the interviews offered participants the opportunity to introduce themselves and included an ice-breaker activity where the young men were asked to share the last TikTok or online video that made them laugh. This was followed by a brief overview of the study and its ethical protocols. The interview questions then prompted participants to speak about:

- which social networking and media sites they used and why;
- who they connected with most online;
- what they mostly did online;
- what motivated them to go online and offline;
- what drew them to particular online spaces or communities;
- when, why and how they might use anonymous identities or personas online;
- when, why and how they post online;
- their general thoughts about posting;
- their thoughts about sharing intimate images online;
- their thoughts about online influencers such as Andrew Tate;
- their thoughts about how their behaviours and beliefs might be shaped by their online experiences;
- how their online experiences impact on their wellbeing and self-esteem; and
- what it means to have a positive experience online.

Given their broadness, these questions opened up discussion on a range of different topics which meant that some topics that were raised and explored in some focus groups were not raised and explored in others. The youth researchers took a participant-centred approach in encouraging discussion when the dynamics of the group expressed particular interest in topics (e.g., such as the toxicity of gaming culture) while mindful of sticking to the interview questions.

Data Analysis and Theoretical Framework

The data were analysed to highlight dominant and recurring themes and were organised in relation to the important issues raised in the research literature presented earlier. To these ends, the analysis that follows articulates the positive and negative aspects of young men's online engagements. It sheds light on the complex ways in which the young men engaged with online spaces as sources of connection, validation and empowerment, on the one hand, and vulnerability, anxiety and harm, on the other. The analysis is feminist-informed (or gender-just) in highlighting how the young men's online encounters challenge and reproduce restrictive and harmful gendered norms and expectations (Henry et al., 2021).

The data analysis is scaffolded by a focus on the young men's critical digital dispositions in their online engagements. The concept of *critical digital dispositions* (Pangrazio, 2018) offers a productive theoretical framework for understanding these engagements by highlighting the significance of four key dimensions: curatorial intentionality, scepticism, ethical engagement and reflexivity. Each dimension is defined below (as it relates to the focus of this book on gender justice—we note that these dispositions may be defined slightly differently elsewhere).

Critical Digital Dispositions Framework

Curatorial intentionality is about the deliberate and intentional process of navigating, filtering and selecting online content to align with particular wants, needs, values and purposes. It is also about the capacity to curate the self in ways that are sensitive to the affordances and audiences of different platforms (Pangrazio, 2018; Weinstein & James, 2022). Intentionality in the process of curating content to consume or create is an act of agency—and indicates a willingness to engage with, and potentially transform, dominant social discourses (Stenalt, 2021). In relation to gender justice, curatorial intentionality would be evident in young men's critical awareness of the equity implications involved in their navigation, filtering and selection of content to consume and create—e.g., the extent to which such intentionality challenges or reproduces restrictive and harmful gendered norms and expectations.

Scepticism involves questioning the assumptions and biases embedded in online content including the architectures (e.g., platform affordances and algorithms) that encourage different kinds of engagements (Pangrazio, 2018). Such scepticism creates a critical awareness of manipulative tactics like clickbait and misinformation (Henderson et al., 2020; Santos-Meneses, 2021). Scepticism is integral to how curatorial intentionality is mobilised because it shapes intentionality. In relation to gender justice, scepticism would be evident in young men's questioning of the gendered online content (e.g., how women are portrayed in online pornography) and architectures (e.g., how algorithms curate their online content in gendered ways) that shape their understandings of gender identities and relations.

Ethical engagement is a process of ongoing action and transformation in relation to what an individual understands to be important and good for themselves and others (Jenkins in Keddie et al., 2021). It is about accepting responsibility and accountability for one's actions and how they impact others (Keddie et al., 2021). Ethical engagement (what is understood to be important and good) shapes how curatorial intentionality and scepticism are enacted. In relation to gender justice, ethical engagement would be evident in young men's awareness and acceptance of responsibility for how actions such as non-consensual sexting may harm others.

Reflexivity is an ongoing process of questioning and challenging issues of personal positionality. It is about adopting a self-critical stance in examining how our biases and prejudices (about gender, sexuality, race, class and ability) shape who and how we are (Keddie et al., 2021). Reflexivity informs the other dimensions in so far as it entails reflecting on how personal positionality shapes curatorial intentionality, scepticism and ethical engagement. In relation to gender justice, reflexivity involves critical consideration of how personal experiences with gender influence interpretations of digital content (e.g., awareness that young men's greater consumption and acceptance of pornography in comparison to young women's concerns about pornography (Martellozzo et al., 2016) relates to gendered positionality and men's greater tendencies to normalise the dominant tropes of pornography).

This framework and the research literature is drawn on in each chapter to make sense of the young men's critical engagement with online spaces. It highlights, in particular, the ways in which the young men support and resist the digital cultures that promote rigid ideas and enactments of gender and masculinity.

Chapter Outlines

Chapter 2: Navigating Leisure, Work and Identity Online

This chapter examines the tensions involved in the young men's navigation of leisure, work and identity online. It explores how young men derive pleasure from the entertainment and social connection online spaces offer but also their concerns about their overuse of online media as unproductive and taking them away from more meaningful activities. The chapter foregrounds the young men's intentional curation of online identities to express different aspects of themselves for different audiences, their anxieties about gendered pressures relating to body image and life milestone expectations, and the affordances and harms of online anonymity. Interspersed within the chapter are analytic summaries that draw attention to how the young men are engaging with curatorial intentionality, scepticism, ethical engagement and reflexivity (Pangrazio, 2018).

Chapter 3: Connection, Community and Conflict

In this chapter the focus is on connection, community and conflict. It explores how the young men derive a sense of belonging, acceptance and support through social media and gaming experiences where they forge positive connections and communities. It also explores how these same communities can be harmful and abusive, prompting some of the young men to disengage and opt out. The chapter highlights how young men's critical engagement in these spaces extends beyond the content they encounter to the architecture of specific online platforms, such as Twitter (X), which are recognised as promoting polarisation and hostility. The chapter provides analytic summaries throughout to highlight how the young men are engaging with the four critical digital dispositions (Pangrazio, 2018).

Chapter 4: Being Led Astray or Misinformed

This chapter explores the young men's concerns about being led astray or misinformed online. These concerns are associated with the negative influence of algorithms shaping their online experiences. Many of the young men expressed scepticism about the ways in which algorithms steer them towards unwelcome or harmful content. In relation to misinformation, the chapter examines the young men's views about credible and false information online, their embracing but also scepticism of the gendered content peddled by the controversial influencer Andrew Tate, and their thoughts about freedom of expression, cancel culture and censorship. The analytic summaries interspersed within the chapter, draw attention to practices of curatorial intentionality, scepticism, ethical engagement and reflexivity (Pangrazio, 2018).

Chapter 5: Sex, Intimacy and Privacy

This chapter examines sex, intimacy and privacy. It foregrounds the young men's concerns about the accessibility and consumption of online pornography in relation to its ubiquity and infiltration in their everyday online experiences. The young men present an overwhelmingly negative picture of how online pornography impacts on their lives including struggles with addiction and the degrading of their relationships with girls and women. The chapter also foregrounds the young men's concerns about privacy and safety online, noting issues ranging from online scams targeting family members to personal encounters with catfishing and the tensions they experience navigating the regulation and censorship of online content. As with the other chapters, this chapter includes analytic summaries to highlight the young men's engagement with critical digital dispositions (Pangrazio, 2018).

Chapter 6: Cultivating Critical Digital Dispositions for Gender Justice

This chapter draws together the findings and insights from the research to highlight the significance of fostering young men's critical digital dispositions for gender justice. The first part of the chapter considers the study's findings in relation to a gender justice framing of the four critical digital dispositions informing the book's analysis: curatorial intentionality, scepticism, ethical engagement and reflexivity. It articulates how the young men's online engagements both support and hinder gender justice—i.e., how their online encounters both challenge and reproduce restrictive and harmful gendered norms. The second part of the chapter provides a series of activity ideas aimed at strengthening these gender justice or feminist-aligned dispositions. The final section of this chapter recognises the need for broader action on the part of policymakers and technology companies working together to create better frameworks that protect individuals from harm and foster ethical online behaviour.

References

APS. (2024). Australian teens trapped by social media apps as the 'like' button triggers mental health disorders. https://psychology.org.au/about-us/news-and-media/aps-in-the-media/2024/australian-teens-trapped-by-social-media-apps-as-t#:~:text=More%20than%20four%20in%2010,%E2%80%9309%20to%202021%E2%80%9322

Baker, C., Ging, D., & Brandt Andreasen, M. (2024). Recommending toxicity: The role of algorithmic recommender functions on YouTube Shorts and TikTok in promoting male supremacist influencers. https://antibullyingcentre.ie/wp-content/uploads/2024/04/DCU-Recommending-Toxicity-Summary-Report.pdf

Bates, L. (2021). *Men who hate women.* Simon & Schuster.

Botto, M., & Gottzén, L. (2023). Swallowing and spitting out the red pill: Young men, vulnerability, and radicalization pathways in the manosphere. *Journal of Gender Studies, 33*(5), 596–608. https://doi.org/10.1080/09589236.2023.2260318

Brito, P., Hayes, C., Lehrer, R., Mahler, J., & Salinas Groppo, J. (2024). *The manosphere, rewired: Understanding masculinities online & pathways for healthy connection.* Equimundo.

Byron, P., Robards, B., Hanckel, B., Vivienne, S., & Churchill, B. (2019). "Hey, i'm having these experiences": Tumblr use and young people's queer (dis)connections. *International Journal of Communication, 13*, 2239–2259.

Dekker, A., Wenzlaff, F., Daubmann, A., Pinnschmidt, H. O., & Briken, P. (2019). (Don't) look at me! How the assumed consensual or non-consensual distribution affects perception and evaluation of sexting images. *Journal of Clinical Medicine, 8*(5), 706.

Drioli-Phillips, P. G., Oxlad, M., LeCouteur, A., Feo, R., & Scholz, B. (2021). Men's talk about anxiety online: Constructing an authentically anxious identity allows help-seeking. *Psychology of Men & Masculinities, 22*(1), 77–87.

Ellis, L., Kathryn, M., Kitty, R., Nicholas, M., Davenport, T., Burns, J., & Hickie, I. (2014). Encouraging young men's participation in mental health research and treatment: Perspectives in our technological age. *Clinical Investigation, 4*(10), 881–888.

Equimundo. (2024). What is the manosphere? https://www.equimundo.org/what-is-the-manosphere/

eSafety Commission. (2023). Accidental, unsolicited and in your face: Young people's encounters with online pornography: A matter of platform responsibility, education and choice. https://apo.org.au/node/324428

eSafety Commissioner. (2021). The digital lives of Aussie teens. https://www.esafety.gov.au/sites/default/files/2021-02/The%20digital%20lives%20of%20Aussie%20teens.pdf?v=1739413907704

eSafety Commissioner. (2024). *Being a young man online: Tensions, complexities and possibilities.* https://www.esafety.gov.au/sites/default/files/2024-06/Being-a-young-man-online-June-2024.pdf?v=1739413767503

Flood, M. (2024). *Media: Porn, online misogyny driving gendered violence.* https://research.qut.edu.au/centre-for-justice/2024/04/30/media-porn-online-misogyny-driving-gendered-violence-professor-michael-flood/

Geena Davis Institute, Oak Foundation, & Equimundo. (2021). *The double edged sword of online gaming: An analysis of masculinity in video games and the gaming community.* Geena Davis Institute, Oak Foundation & Equimundo.

Ging, D. (2019). Alphas, betas, and incels: Theorizing the masculinities of the manosphere. *Men and Masculinities, 22*(4), 638–657.

Ging, D., & Siapera, E. (2018). Special issue on online misogyny. *Feminist Media Studies, 18*(4), 515–524.

Henderson M. J., Shade L. R., Mackinnon K. (2020). Every click you make: Algorithmic literacy and the digital lives of young adults. AoIR Selected Papers of Internet Research. https://doi.org/10.5210/spir.v2020i0.11233

Haslop, C., Ringrose, J., Cambazoglu, I., & Milne, B. (2024). Mainstreaming the manosphere's misogyny through affective homosocial currencies. *Social Media & Society, 10*(1), 1. https://doi.org/10.1177/20563051241228811

Henry, N., Stefani, V., & Alice, W. (2021). Digital citizenship in a global society: A feminist approach. *Feminist Media Studies, 22*(8), 1972–1989.

Hunt, G., & Higgins, D. (2024). Deepfake AI pornography is becoming more common—What can parents and schools do to prevent it? *The Conversation.* https://theconversation.com/deepfake-ai-pornography-is-becoming-more-common-what-can-parents-and-schools-do-to-prevent-it-232248

Kaye, B., & Menon, P. (2024). *Australia passes social media ban for children under 16.* Reuters.

Keddie, A., Hewson-Munro, S., Halafoff, A., Delaney, M., & Flood, M. (2022). Programmes for boys and men: Possibilities for gender transformation. *Gender and Education, 35*(3), 250–266.

Keddie, A., Lees, D., & Delaney, M. (2021). Reflexivity, ethics and accountability: Facilitators working for gender transformation with boys and men. *Journal of Gender Studies, 32*(3), 259–269. https://doi.org/10.1080/09589236.2021.1990031

Koester, D., & Marcus, R. (2024). *How does social media influence gender norms among adolescent boys?* https://www.alignplatform.org/sites/default/files/2024-03/align-socialmedia-report-feb24-proof04.pdf

Liu, O. (2022). *Effects of hypermasculine and heteronormative elements in video games on gender role beliefs among young adult males and comparisons to sex-positive media.* https://osf.io/preprints/socarxiv/9w642

Maloney, M., Roberts, S., & Jones, C. (2022). "How do I become blue pilled?": Masculine ontological insecurity on 4c Han's advice board. *New Media & Society, 26*(6), 3307–3326.

Martellozzo, E., Monaghan, A., Adler, J. R., Davidson, J., Leyva, R., & Horvath, M. A. (2016). *"I wasn't sure it was normal to watch it…" a quantitative and qualitative examination of the impact of online pornography on the values, attitudes, beliefs and behaviours of children and young people.* Middlesex University, NSPCC, OCC.

Palmér, L. (2015). "Poppin' bottles, getting wheysted." Exploring young men's engagement with fitspiration content and its consequential influences on attitudes and behaviour. *Journal of Promotional Communications, 3*, 425–445.

Pangrazio, L. (2018). *Young people's literacies in the digital age: Continuities, conflicts and contradictions.* Routledge.

Plan International. (2020). *Social media is the new frontier for gendered violence, as biggest ever global study of girls' experiences online reveals endemic abuse and harassment.* https://www.plan.org.au/media-centre/social-media-new-frontier-for-gendered-violence-as/

Ravn, S., Coffey, J., & Roberts, S. (2019). The currency of images: Risk, value and gendered power dynamics in young men's accounts of sexting. *Feminist Media Studies, 21*(2), 315–331.

Ringrose, J., Regehr, K., & Whitehead, S. (2021). Teen girls' experiences negotiating the ubiquitous dick pic: Sexual double standards and the normalization of image based sexual harassment. *Sex Roles, 85*, 558–576.

Roberts, S., Jones, C., Nicholas, L., Wescott, S., & Maloney, M. (2025). Beyond the clickbait: Analysing the masculinist ideology in Andrew Tate's online written discourses. *Cultural Sociology.* https://doi.org/10.1177/17499755241307414

Robinson, M., & Robertson, S. (2010). Young men's health promotion and new information communication technologies: Illuminating the issues and research agendas. *Health Promotion International, 25*(3), 363–370.

Santos-Meneses, L. F. (2021). Thinking critically through controversial issues on digital media: Dispositions and key criteria for content evaluation. *Thinking Skills and Creativity, 42*, 100927. https://doi.org/10.1016/j.tsc.2021.100927

Siibak, A. (2010). Constructing masculinity on a social networking site. *Young, 18*(4), 403–425. https://doi.org/10.1177/110330881001800403

Stenalt, M. H. (2021). Digital student agency: Approaching agency in digital contexts from a critical perspective. *Frontline Learning Research, 9*(3), 52–68. https://doi.org/10.14786/flr.v9i3.697

Thomas, A. B., Ross, M., & Harris, K. K. (2007). Coming out online: Interpretations of young men's stories. *Sexuality Research & Social Policy, 4*, 5–17.

Tyler, R. E., & Williams, S. (2014). Masculinity in young men's health: Exploring health, help-seeking and health service use in an online environment. *Journal of Health Psychology, 19*(4), 457–470.

Wack, E., & Tantleff-Dunn, S. (2009). Relationships between electronic game play, obesity, and psychosocial functioning in young men. *Cyberpsychology & Behavior, 12*(2), 241–244.

Wang, V., & Edwards, S. (2016). Strangers are friends I haven't met yet: A positive approach to young people's use of social media. *Journal of Youth Studies, 19*(9), 1204–1219.

Weinstein, E., & James, C. (2022). *Behind their screens: What teens are facing and adults are missing.* The MIT Press.

Wescott, S., Roberts, S., & Zhao, X. (2023). The problem with anti-feminist 'manfluencer' Andrew Tate in Australian schools: Women teachers' experiences of resurgent male supremacy. *Gender & Education, 36*(2), 167–182.

CHAPTER 2

Navigating Leisure, Work and Identity Online

Abstract This chapter examines the tensions involved in young men's navigation of leisure, work and identity online. It explores how young men derive pleasure from the entertainment, social connection and professional development online spaces offer but also their concerns about their overuse of online media as unproductive and taking them away from more meaningful activities. The chapter notes their struggles with the addictive nature of social media platforms and their critical awareness of the platform design and algorithms that encourage overuse. The discussion foregrounds the young men's intentional curation of online identities to express different aspects of themselves for different audiences, influenced by broader ideals of self-improvement. It highlights their mixed feelings about the male empowerment messages promoted by social media influencer Andrew Tate as both positive and negative. The discussion also foregrounds the young men's anxieties about gendered pressures relating to body image, life milestone expectations and the affordances and harms of online anonymity. Interspersed within the chapter are analytic summaries that draw attention to how the young men are engaging with curatorial intentionality, scepticism, ethical engagement and reflexivity [Pangrazio, L. (2018). *Young people's literacies in the digital age: Continuities, conflicts and contradictions*. Routledge].

A. Keddie, M. Flood, *Young Men's Online Lives*,
https://doi.org/10.1007/978-3-031-99980-2_2

Keywords Young men • Leisure • Work • Identity • Online engagements • Overuse of social media • Gendered pressures

Online Engagements as Pleasurable and Useful

The young men highlighted the many positive aspects of their online experiences which encompassed a spectrum of entertainment, personal interests, knowledge acquisition, and engagement in study- and work-related activities. The young men drew on and navigated a range of different online applications and platforms for these purposes.

Entertainment and fun were key motivations associated with the young men's online experiences (eSafety Commissioner, 2021). Many spoke of seeking out entertainment on applications such as TikTok, as Daniel (19, G) explained: "I use Tik Tok ... it just kind of releases that serotonin [and] makes you kind of happy ... if you watch all those funny videos." Bailey (16, S, CALD) and Tim (17, S, CALD) echoed this sentiment, with both expressing their enjoyment of TikTok videos. Aaron (19, S) emphasised the role of entertainment, whether it be for "a laugh" or the discovery of "fun facts". For Maxie (21, S, CALD), the internet involves having access to "that constancy of entertainment, especially after a long day of work", and "it just feels great". Others viewed online documentaries as key entertainment material. Warren (18, S) noted that he often has a documentary playing during his recreational time, while Quinn's (20, S) interests included nature documentaries and sports documentaries. Many of the young men also mentioned their engagement with online gaming as pleasurable and entertaining (gaming will be examined in the next chapter).

The young men expressed enthusiasm for accessing online content related to their sporting interests. Manny (18, S), for example, spoke of watching sporting highlights featuring his favourite football team. Similarly, Majak (21, S, CALD), a "big basketball fan", noted watching basketball in ESPN videos on YouTube. Kenneth (21, S) spoke of discussing sports with his friends, sharing game updates and post-game analysis. He streams a wide range of sports, from football to cricket, accounting for a significant portion of his internet activity. Nate (18, S, CALD) mentioned his engagement with Australian Rules Football (one of Australia's main sporting codes) through Instagram and Facebook groups where he had "a lot of conversation" about the games among his friends. Kristian (21, S, CALD) mentioned that he utilised transit and downtime to browse sports-related subreddits, staying updated on various sports including cricket and rugby league.

Many of the young men spoke of using the internet as a gateway to knowledge and news tailored to their interests (eSafety Commissioner, 2021). They leveraged various digital platforms, from social media to newsletters, YouTube, and TikTok, to satisfy their curiosity, access pertinent news, and engage in learning. Jase (20, S, CALD) spoke of utilising the internet for news trends and research, from keeping abreast of current events to identifying insects in his backyard. Brenton (21, S) highlighted the efficiency of platforms like TikTok for quick information retrieval. Kieran (19, S) mentioned his online strategy of using social media, YouTube, and web searches to access "nerd news" and a wealth of information tailored to his interests. Brodie (20, B) consulted YouTube as a significant learning tool to "stay up to date" with "what's going on in the news" but also because he wanted "to know everything". Other young men similarly noted the utility of being able to search for virtually any topic and obtain "any answer that you need for that specific thing" (Henry, 16, S); the internet as a tool for "research" and "learning" (Simon, 19, Ax); and "learning something new" (Bairam, 18, S, CALD).

In a similar vein, others like Charlie (19, S) commented on the internet's ability to enhance various aspects of their lives, from travel to cooking. Charlie viewed the internet as a tool that enhances his offline experiences by providing valuable information and resources: "I feel like you have the internet as something that can just add to the real world and make it lot better in so many different ways". Felix (20, B) similarly commented that positive experiences online led to enhancing offline experiences such as through "researching about a hike I'm gonna do on the weekends".

The young men mentioned the significance of their online activities for study and work (eSafety Commissioner, 2021). They noted a range of online tools and platforms that enhanced their learning and professional pursuits. Jase (20, S, CALD), for example, spoke of using platforms such as WhatsApp and Zoom to connect with peers, share resources, and discuss coursework which helped to foster his learning. Kenneth (21, S) noted his use of YouTube for tutorial videos and lectures to enhance his knowledge and skills, while Tariq (19, S) found the GenAI tool ChatGPT useful for academic tasks at university. For Danveer (18, S, CALD) a dedicated Discord server was useful for sharing resources and assisting with his homework.

Within the analytic framework of critical digital dispositions, these comments reflect curatorial intentionality (Pangrazio, 2018). The young men demonstrate purposeful and strategic engagement with digital platforms such as TikTok, YouTube, WhatsApp, and Discord, curating content and tools to align with their interests, goals, and values. Their selective use of these platforms for entertainment, learning, and collaboration highlights their agency in tailoring their digital lives to serve their personal interests and development (Stenalt, 2021).

Young Men's Concerns with Overuse of Online Media

While the young men in this research expressed pleasure about their online experiences, they also expressed concerns about their overuse of social and other online media. These concerns were marked by a collective awareness and worry regarding the perceived addictive nature of certain social media platforms and activities. The young men offered a candid and critical examination of the challenges posed by what they viewed as excessive screen time.

As with key research in this space (Adorjan & Ricciardelli, 2021; eSafety Commissioner, 2018), many of the young men expressed concerns about the 'addictive' nature of certain social media apps, especially Tik Tok. Manny (18, S) noted his fears about getting "too addicted" to Tik Tok. He compared this application to Instagram reels, commenting that both can lead to "scrolling into endless oblivion". Similarly, Ibrahim (18, S, CALD) reported that "I don't touch Tik Tok … I find myself like wasting so much time on it like it just, it's never ending. Just keep scrolling, and it's just too much dopamine hits, like it's no good for you", while Felix (20, B) described Tik Tok as a "rabbit hole-y app" given the platform's algorithms work to keep you engaged. Nico (18, S, D, CALD) referred to the use of Tik Tok as an "unproductive habit".

There was a collective critique of excessive social media use and an acknowledgement of the challenges of self-control. Many of the young men expressed a desire to redirect their time towards what they saw as more meaningful and fulfilling activities. When invited in the focus groups to look at their phone data on their daily social media use, Brenton (21, S) and Maxie (21, S, CALD), for example, noted their underestimation of their use and expressed concern about their excessive use as 'embarrassing' and 'unhealthy':

> I'm just checking out [my] daily average on TikTok is five hours. Sorry, that's quite embarrassing. I was gonna say two hours but yeah, that's shocking. But done at night like before bed I reckon. (Brenton, 21, S)

> Yeah, I just had a look at my daily usage on TikTok. I'm averaging three hours a day, which is very unhealthy, I think. I didn't know it was that long ... I tend to watch YouTube just for entertainment reasons, then social media here and there throughout the day ... yeah, my screen time is really bad. (Maxie, 21, S, CALD)

This issue of self-control as a challenge for young people in managing their use of social media has been a focus of recent research (Adorjan & Ricciardelli, 2021). Many of the young men described the design of platforms such as TikTok, YouTube, and Instagram—featuring infinite scrolling, personalised recommendations, and constant notifications—as making it difficult to moderate their time online. (Issues relating to algorithms will be explored in Chap. 4.) The constant allure of online media, combined with the 'fear of missing out' (FOMO) (eSafety Commissioner, 2018; Hefner et al., 2018), exacerbates their difficulty in setting boundaries and sticking to them.

The notion of social media use as unproductive was a common theme for many of the young men. Campbell (18, B, D) spoke negatively of spending hours on apps like Tik Tok and said that this was not intentional but "accidental". He noted the subsequent need to break away to feel productive in life. Similarly, Leslie (17, S) recognised the unproductive nature of his TikTok usage as "taking a big chunk of my free time" and "not productive at all". Nate (18, S, CALD) made a distinction between various forms of entertainment, emphasising that screen-based "entertainment through your phone" feels less "productive" than outdoor activities or reading. Tariq (19, S) mentioned the need to cut down on screen time as part of his "self-improvement" journey. Franklin (21, S) shared his experience of deleting TikTok due to its addictive nature, only to find himself substituting it with other platforms, as he explained: "so I'm still wasting that time irrespective, it's just replacing it with something else ... I'm kind of just wasting away on my computer".

Similarly, Mack (19, U, CALD) expressed frustration at realising how much time he spent on social media instead of engaging in more meaningful activities, stating "I could have done something actually productive in my life". Christian (17, S, D) and Spencer (18, B, CALD) noted their "mindless scrolling" on platforms like TikTok and Instagram as draining productivity while Oliver (21, Q) commented on the allure of platforms like TikTok and Instagram, which curate content and keep users engaged for hours, stating that it undermined his productivity: "yeah, it sucks out my productivity a little bit and I don't love it". Charlie (19, S) expressed "a sense of unhappiness" with his overuse of social media, describing this as an unhappiness "at myself for not us[ing] my time as productively as I can". Nawaz (20, S, CALD) reported engaging in a "doom scrolling" loop, particularly during commutes, indicating how social media can become an unproductive time sink.

Several of the young men expressed awareness of how excessive social media and technology use can have a detrimental impact on their offline connections and experiences, as Toby (16, S) remarked: "If I go on [social media] too much, I feel like I'm just, you know ... just disconnected from the world". Nathan (17, S) similarly noted the importance of going offline to "walk outside and get some fresh air ... [to] clear up your mind and feel less heavy." Toby (16, S) also noted the "sluggish" feeling when he is online for too long. Research in this space consistently draws attention to such concerns, that is, that excessive online (social media) engagement can disrupt offline lives and interfere with essential activities such as studying, physical exercise, and maintaining face-to-face relationships (eSafety Commissioner, 2018).

Consistent with other research in this space, many of the young men spoke of finding it difficult to be away from their devices (Adorjan & Ricciardelli, 2021; Pangrazio, 2018; eSafety Commissioner, 2018). The inability for young people to disconnect or moderate their time online leaves many feeling stuck in patterns they recognise as harmful. Young people report feeling an overwhelming urge to check their social media accounts frequently, driven by 'FOMO' (fear of missing out) on updates or social interactions.

The young men also spoke about excessive internet use as impacting on their satisfaction online. Oliver (21, Q), for example, expressed the feeling of never being satisfied due to endless scrolling, especially during late-night internet sessions. He noted that this pattern can lead to an overwhelming sense of information overload: "I just keep thinking I need to know more and more and it's just neverending. It can be overwhelming in that sense. Like never satisfied". Kristian (21, S, CALD) mentioned that his social media use was akin to “instant muscle memory [to] go back into the app … it’s like passively consuming something and it reaches a point where you’re just like. This isn’t even that entertaining for me. So, it’s like, why am I doing it?” Similarly, Nawaz (20, S, CALD) mentioned that he could “tell” when he had “had too much [of social media] when it comes to the point where none of it is entertaining [him] anymore”.

Several of the young men noted that their overuse of social media, and particularly its distracting effect, negatively impacted on their academic studies, as other scholarship has documented (Dontre, 2020). Manny (18, S), for example, spoke of “cut[ting] down on [his] screen time” to prioritise his final year of secondary school studies, as he explained: “I tried to put my goal of like getting into Uni above all these Instagram reels and everything”. Devon (21, S) deleted Tik Tok because his excessive use was impacting on his studies, while Omer (17, S, CALD) and Julian (19, S, CALD) both recognised the need to reduce their social media usage during periods of increased focus, such as studying for exams.

Consistent with research (Samari et al., 2022) that draws attention to young people’s efforts to develop more balanced internet habits, other young men in this study commented further on the proactive steps they took to curb their social media use. Charlie (19, S) put a “YouTube blocker” on his computer to control his use of this app. Bairam (18, S, CALD) used a “minimalist” app for Instagram to time his usage and “get rid of his scrolling addiction”, while Benito (20, S, CALD) emphasised the importance of self-control and monitoring app usage: “if I wanna sort of monitor it or like fully control it, I’ll just delete whatever apps I wanna delete … that’s sort of a good measure, a good way to sort of control things”.

Beyond personal struggles, some of the young men expressed concern about how excessive internet use affects younger generations. Felix (20, B) voiced concerns about the impact of “brain rot content” on youth, as he commented: “look, I grew up with the internet, and I’m pretty hooked on it but people who are younger than me like, if this is what they’re like going straight into that’s … that’s absolutely terrifying to me”. Hugh (20, S) expressed unease about younger generations in light of the rapid judgments and constant stimulation they face from a young age. Additionally, Dev (19, S, CALD) noted his concern about how some young people “can’t be without the internet at all … from the time they wake up to the time they go to bed”.

Curatorial intentionality is evident in this section in the young men's attempts to moderate their social media use. Such attempts involve employing app blockers or deleting applications to regain control over their screen time. These actions demonstrate curatorial agency, as they consciously shape their digital habits to align with personal priorities, such as productivity and meaningful offline interactions. The young men's critique of manipulative platform features, including infinite scrolling and algorithm-driven content, highlights their scepticism about how these technological structures foster addictive behaviours. This critical awareness indicates their understanding of how digital environments influence user actions (Pangrazio, 2018; Santos-Meneses, 2021). However, there is a conflict between the young men's efforts to curate their online experiences and the technological structures that foster engagement. While they express a strong desire to moderate their engagement, many struggle with the addictive design of platforms. This struggle highlights the broader issue of digital control, where individual agency is constantly challenged by platform mechanics. It also highlights the young men's struggles for more ethical online engagements—i.e., that are more consistent with their ideas of what is important and good for themselves and others. A significant concern here is how the young men accept personal responsibility for managing these conflicts absolving the responsibility of online platforms to mitigate compulsive design features (Pangrazio, 2018).

Expressing Different Aspects of Identity for Different Audiences

Many of the young men in this research reported making use of online spaces to express different aspects of their identities. Consistent with other research (Dyer, 2015; Pangrazio, 2018), the young men used various online platforms to express different aspects of their identity, tailoring their self-presentation for different audiences. The young men used the affordances of social media to shape how they expressed themselves, what content or thoughts they shared, and with whom (Dyer, 2015).

In relation to posting online, for example, Campbell (18, B, D) noted, "there is certainly a divide between what you want your parents to see and what you want your friends [to see]. The really weird like Instagram like memes and stuff that you might put on your story … it wouldn't necessarily be good for [your] parents to see." Presenting different aspects of identity for different audiences was a common theme across many of the interviews. Chen (18, G, CALD) stated simply that he was a "bit more loud with my friends" and "just like closed off" with family. Similarly, Franklin (21, S) noted, "With friends, I'm a bit more out there and I'll react with like angry faces and stuff like that a bit more, but with family it's much more conservative, just love heart reactions". Lucas (18, S) managed the tension between posting for parents and friends by having dual accounts, one for his friends and one for family. This reflects a type of 'self-curatorship' that digital media researchers argue is typical of the production and representation of identities online (Potter, 2012; Pangrazio, 2018).

The use of privacy settings, in a similar vein to multiple accounts, was seen as enabling the young men to ensure a select audience to communicate different aspects of themselves. Nate (18, S, CALD) spoke here of creating "second private accounts" to share "inside jokes" with close friends "who would understand them", while Campbell (18, B, D) spoke of creating specific accounts for "really obscure stuff" for people who "understand you better, like they know what type of content you would associate yourself with".

Kenneth (21, S) distinguished between his public face that may be viewed by employers and his private space: "if people are going to look you up online, they're probably gonna look you up on Facebook first, or LinkedIn maybe, if you're really businessy but they, my Instagram accounts [have] always been private". Jamie (16, First Nations) also distinguished between his public and private online spaces, noting the different ways he presented himself in these different spaces:

> I keep all my business on [my business account] … I restrict it to that … I've noticed the way I interact with people is very different on that account compared to how I am normally, and I find on there, because it's, because I am representing myself as a business … I definitely go about what I say very carefully. (Jamie, 16, First Nations)

The young men's accounts of how they expressed themselves online for different audiences noted the issue of authenticity. Toby (16, S) confided that he felt he could be "more honest" and "genuine" online with his family and close friends than with his broader circle of friends. Referring to Facebook, Lleyton (16, S) similarly felt he could be more himself on this platform because he trusted the people with whom he interacted, as he explained: "no one's gonna post something bad or yeah, negative about me … just who I have on there [are] just people I can really trust." (Lleyton, 16, S).

Consistent with this comment, some of the young men noted how online spaces allowed more freedom of expression than offline spaces, as Geoffrey (20, G, CALD) noted: "I think the people [who] are generally maybe inhibited in person or they have their guard up a little bit and so I think they feel a little bit freer on the internet to expressing a little bit more, be a bit more loose." Omer (17, S, CALD) similarly noted that he tended to "find out a lot more about" his friends in "private chats" than in face-to-face contact. Franklin (21, S) spoke of feeling freer to be himself in online spaces, attributing this to being able to be anonymous (we explore the issue of anonymity in more detail later in the book):

> I feel like I'm a lot more conservative in my day-to-day life as opposed to when I'm online, I'm a bit more, I feel more comfortable saying my opinion. Well, it's not face to face and it's under an online persona as opposed to my name and they can't see me and you know, it's behind the screen. I feel more comfortable saying opinions that other people may not like and it's not anything racist or outrageous, it's just, you know, I can actually say what I'm thinking as opposed to being more concerned, what do they think, you know? (Franklin, 21, S)

The critical digital disposition of curatorial intentionality is evident here in the young men's deliberate management of their online identities and self-presentation for different audiences. Many strategically use dual accounts to separate interactions with friends, family, or employers, enabling them to navigate varied social expectations. This form of digital self-curation demonstrates their agency in managing and controlling their online presence and their ability to align digital engagement with personal goals and values (Pangrazio, 2018; Santos-Meneses, 2021). Such curation seems to be driven by the young men's desire for ethical engagement—i.e., what they view as important and good for themselves and others. This is evident in their contemplation of authenticity and self-expression in their curatorial intentionality to respond to the greater comfort they feel sharing opinions online (rather than offline) where anonymity and trusted networks allow for greater openness and genuine-ness (with close friends and family in private digital spaces). A desire for ethical engagement is also evident in their cautious use of privacy settings and careful management of their digital accounts to establish appropriate boundaries and prevent misunderstandings.

Shaping Identities Through Self-Improvement Content

The content the young men sought out in their online engagement was illuminating in relation to issues of identity. The young men actively sought out content associated with self-improvement and male empowerment in trying to be the best version of themselves, including materials associated with maximising physical fitness, body image (Palmér, 2015) and personal finances (Feltham, 2024).

For some of the young men, the online world is a space for general self-improvement, a means to 'better yourself'. Influencers—individuals on social media with social influence—were seen by many of the young men as an important source of self-improvement and inspiration. Maxie (21, S, CALD) offered praise for influencers: "some of the values that they do try and impart like basic discipline, trying to be what a man should be, I would say that is actually slightly good". Majak (21, S, CALD) agreed, referring to content by Kobe Bryant, an American former professional basketball player, as supporting him to learn "a lot of practical, real-world solutions to issues and problems" he faced during covid lockdown.

Andrew Tate, a very well-known and controversial American-British media influencer and self-proclaimed misogynist, was nominated by some of the young men as an important source of inspiration for general self-improvement (Keddie et al., 2024). Influencers such as Tate are particularly popular: in an Australian poll among 1374 young men in late 2022, 92% knew of Andrew Tate, 35% agreed that he was relatable, while 25% agreed that they look up to Tate as a role model (The Man Cave, 2023). The male empowerment narratives presented by influencers such as Andrew Tate shape the expressions of identity among young men, influencing their views on what being a man is, or should be, around traditional ideas of masculinity. This perspective suggests that some young men are resistant to shifting gender norms and wish to reaffirm traditional male roles.

Several of the young men spoke of Tate's positive influence on their sense of self. Manny (18, S) said, "I haven't watched heaps of [Andrew Tate's] stuff, but like, from what I've seen, [he] has inspired me in setting ways to just become a better person all around". Drew (16, S, D, CALD) said, "I haven't watched like every single video that he has, but, like the occasional few, has given me maybe a bit more confidence." Warren (18, S) too described Tate as inspiring self-improvement: "I'm quite supportive of lots of things [Tate says] … Just being the best version of yourself is stuff that I've started to live by". Some of the young men endorsed the male empowerment narratives of Tate because they felt he makes points about gender relations that have otherwise been unsaid or silenced:

> I've watched a lot of this stuff and … I agree with most of it. […] this … guy's putting out so many opinions of things that haven't been said in ages because of feminist movements and everything … he's the only one speaking out about this sort of male stuff that's not spoken about. (Brenton, 21, S)

Along these lines, some of the young men viewed Andrew Tate as a legitimate advocate for male empowerment, in a context where female empowerment has been too much the focus and males now, according to Brenton (21, S), have "no chance" for empowerment (Feltham, 2024). Jase agreed:

> [Andrew Tate is] try[ing] to instil traditional human male masculinity into today's generation of men … he protects his partner, you know, all the good stuff as well … but in terms of the whole equality thing, I think, the whole social movement has gotten a little extreme and it's essentially the women's empowerment movement, they're trying to not exactly replace us, but kind of. (Jase, 20, S, CALD)

Some of the young men expressed the view that Tate's male empowerment message was particularly important in a context where young men have few positive role models and there has been a 'large focus away from masculinity', as Nico (18, S, D, CALD) commented:

> There aren't many, you know, strong male kind of role models for younger, for younger men growing up, you see, you know, like feminism is getting … like popular and stuff. It's getting quite strong […] that's cool. That's very cool. I, you know, you love to see that stuff. However, you see, like there's been a large focus away from like masculinity and stuff. And I think Andrew Tate, he [plays] an important role in reminding us, you know, what we should try [to strive] towards.

Tate's video-clip-based media is notorious for its misogynist and violence-supportive content, but his written content, likely to be consumed by more loyal fans, is more subtle. Quantitative analysis of the writings on Tate's website and Telegram channel finds that 89% of the text focuses on men and masculinity, and only 11% on women and femininity (Roberts et al., 2025). Most of Tate's written content is focused on advancing particular projections of manhood, centred on material wealth, physical strength and aggression, sexual prowess, and social recognition. Although little of this material centres on overt hostility to women, his writings nevertheless naturalise gender hierarchies and frame men ideally as dominant over women (Roberts et al., 2025).

The young men's engagements with male empowerment narratives shaped their expressions of identity especially in relation to physical fitness and body image. Consistent with the notion of 'fitspiration' outlined in Palmér's work (2015), the young men's selection of influencers in this space was closely related to an idealised masculinity of physical strength, endurance and muscularity. There were other influencers the young men mentioned in this respect such as retired United States Navy SEAL and ultramarathon runner David Goggins. Goggins was viewed as inspiring ongoing involvements in physical activity, as Kenneth (21, S) explained:

> David Goggins is a guy that I listen to when I'm running a fair bit as well, because that man is a freak … it's those sort of guys … that I listen to that have some sort of way of putting into practice every single day and finding motivation every single day in repetition that I'm like, yeah, that's something I want to get into. (Kenneth, 21, S)

For one young man, online information on 'looksmaxing'—on how to maximise one's physical appearance or looks for personal gain—was an important form of self-improvement, including after experiencing relationship rejection:

> It's a funny story. I got a bad haircut, and my crush rejected me, so I was like, what the hell, you know … am I [not] desirable or something? I did a bit of research on like, okay, how do I, you know, make myself better? … I stumbled across where they had like a lot of new terms that I've never heard of like looksmaxing and all of that. It's getting really popular nowadays, but it's about, you know, how can I make myself better? And then I was like showing the standards that you have to fit to […] just the casual things: hitting the gym more, doing more exercise and feeling good about myself. (Bairam, 18, S, CALD)

These comments about self-improvement resonate with a new form of masculinity introduced by philosopher Andrew Taggart, what he calls the 'secular monk'. This version of masculinity is characterised by deliberate solitude, rigorous self-discipline and a dedication to personal optimisation and self-sufficiency, often at the expense of forming deep interpersonal relationships (Thompson, 2025). Daily routines, as depicted in various media, typically emphasise solitary activities aimed at enhancing physical health, mental clarity, and financial success. This lifestyle reflects a broader societal trend toward increased individualism and reduced social engagement. Taggart's analysis suggests that this movement represents a significant shift in contemporary masculinity, where the focus on self-optimisation leads to a form of voluntary isolation (Thompson, 2025).

As part of the self-improvement narrative, much of the young men's engagement with influencers centred on making money (Feltham, 2024). For several young men, Andrew Tate provided them with such knowledge. Drew (16, S, D, CALD) commented that, "[Tate] can motivate men. He encourages people to try and make money [and] all that." Derek (20, S, CALD) noted that, "a few things that I did get from Tate, making money, as a lot of us did and that got me interested in personal finance". Brenton (21, S) and Warren (18, S) too praised Tate's financial acumen:

> I've got a couple of small businesses and like the amount of information that I've got from [Andrew Tate] … there's just genuinely like amazing knowledge to have … he's got a bunch of good ideas. (Brenton, 21, S)

> … since I started following him. I've made probably three times more money than I did before. I'm in the best physical shape I've been in my entire life and I just kind of have a better perception of the world. (Warren, 18, S)

Quantitative analysis of Andrew Tate's written content echoes these themes, finding that it emphasises wealth and power as central to masculinity, reflecting conventional and long-standing signifiers of a successful masculinity (Roberts et al., 2025). Tate stresses that wealth alone is insufficient: men must also be physically powerful and proficient in combat.

Although Tate's narratives of self-improvement may seem less troubling than his more overt misogynistic pronouncements, they also can contribute to ideological support for patriarchal inequalities. Analysis of Tate's writings documents that they promote a vision of men as protectors and rulers over women and women as living ideally in the service of men, as wives, mothers and carers. Desirable women must take a submissive and subservient position to men, while men must 'care for' them as a 'sacred duty' (Roberts et al., 2025).

There were also several voices of disinterest or criticism regarding influencers and the people who follow them. As Dev (19, S, CALD) commented, "I basically don't like, follow influencers. I think most … 99 percent of them are fake … just do it to get payment, recognition … it makes me think, these idiots are just wasting their life trying to follow, somebody like, non-genuine." Felix (20, B) criticised male influencers' narrow focus on physical outcomes and financial success, noting their neglect of emotional wellbeing and other dimensions of a good life. He commented:

> [Male influencers] just don't necessarily represent what being a man is all about like, it doesn't actually necessarily represent what you should be striving to be as a person, you know, like it's not promoting emotional kind of sensitivity or an understanding of like, you know, your mental health. A lot of it focuses on, you know, physical outcomes, monetary outcomes. It's very objective. And those are all things that are fine. But they don't necessarily promote, like, a life that will be enjoyable to live. (Felix, 20, B)

Other young men in the study were highly critical of Andrew Tate (Keddie et al., 2024; eSafety Commissioner, 2024). Several drew on feminist and ethical discourses in criticising Tate's views of women and gender and his hypocritical, unethical and criminal behaviour. Tristan (18, S) emphasised his disagreement with Tate's "stupid" claim that men are better than women:

> I'd say he could be pretty far out there like, I think I remember seeing a clip of him saying, like men are better than women. I do think they should be equal, because I can see sometimes that men treat women unequally, and I don't see why, we're all people and I've seen many clips have been saying that they are better than women … I think it's just a bit like stupid. (Tristan, 18, S)

Lionel (20, S) was scathing about Tate. In a long critique, he noted the contradictions between Tate's words and his actions: "he really wants to be a loving father and he really respects the women in his life, but [he] also runs a freaking [human] trafficking ring", "he's going on about how he doesn't own anybody, but he's getting arrested for literally owning and stealing money off of webcam models", he "switch[ed] from being Christian [to Muslim]. Proclaiming a lot of Christian values to being a Muslim very quickly. What does that say?" Jase (20, S, CALD) too was deeply critical of Tate, highlighting Tate's justifications for cheating on his partners as "not cheating" but "exercise", his focus on "how much money he's got and how many girls he's been with" and his alleged trafficking. As such, Jase noted, "I don't really wanna consume his content."

Other young men stated their general dislike for or discomfort with Andrew Tate and or his views. Kyle (18, S, CALD) said, "he can make some good points, but you know he also makes a lot of really bad choices ... a lot of people are really against him and, you know, I am also one of the people that don't really like him" while Felix (20, B) stated that one form of online content that makes him feel uncomfortable involves:

> specific people and personalities so, influencers who are, you know, whether it just be the way they are or if they're acting for their online persona, kind of stir shit [make trouble for other people or drama] and act out and say outrageous things to get attention. People like Andrew Tate, perfect example, just like the things that he says make me so uncomfortable. It's just gross and it's for attention and it gets, and it gets the attention of the media. (Felix, 20, B)

Several of the young men expressed concern about the negative impact Tate was having on younger, more impressionable boys and young men. They emphasised that younger males are more naïve and easily influenced than older males, and thus more vulnerable to negative influences from commentators such as Tate. Geoffrey (20, G, CALD) stated, for example, "I think it's super concerning where like especially younger guys are going ... the concerning part is that they're naive." Likewise, Ren (19, S, CALD) reported that in talking to his friends:

> we kind of realised that it's really easy to be like, convinced, and like kind of be manipulated [in a] way, just like you kind of lose your thoughts ... for younger generations especially, I think it'd be like really easy for them to be manipulat[ed] ... just like that is the right thing to do, and that should be the way you should be and you can forget the values in between that process. ... gotta be careful is what I kinda realised. (Ren, 19, S, CALD)

Vincent (21, S) suggested that Tate is adept at being an influential male role model for impressionable boys and young men who lack these:

> it definitely like targets, like 13 year-olds who like they're growing up on the internet ... they're figuring, like, what does it mean to be a man? And then there's this guy who's really very cool. He's like, you know, destroying all the feminists, or he goes on a podcast. He's really cool ... he was kinda smart because he was like taking advantage of all these impressionable young people who may [need] another male role model in their life. ... I definitely get why people get sucked into it. (Vincent, 21, S)

The young men's critical digital dispositions in this section are reflected in their selective engagement with online content, particularly in self-improvement and empowerment, highlighting the importance of curatorial intentionality. By purposefully seeking out influencers and material that align with their aspirations, such as enhancing physical fitness, financial literacy, or personal confidence, they demonstrate agency in shaping their digital experiences. For example, those who found inspiration in figures like Kobe Bryant or David Goggins exhibit a clear intent to adopt values such as discipline and perseverance. Such intentionality might be seen as an ethical engagement in this online material to the extent that they are seeking out content that is important and good for them—the secular monk version of masculinity aptly captures an ethics of self-discipline and self-sufficiency that is good and important for these young men. The positive comments about Tate, relating to speaking out for men in a world where feminism is taking over, might also be seen as an ethical statement from the position of these young men. However, ethical engagement is also about considering what is important and good for others and accepting responsibility for how one's actions impact on others. In this sense, the young men's ethical engagement here is limited.

In the second part of this section, in contrast, we see a level of reflexivity and self-critique in the young men's ethical engagements with influencer content. They express scepticism about the authenticity of influencers and their narrow focus on physical outcomes and financial success, they critique the narrow version of masculinity promoted by some influencers that lacks emotional sensitivity, and they draw on feminist and ethical discourses to challenge Tate's views of women and gender. Such scepticism is mobilised in ethical and reflexive ways towards gender justice—i.e., a questioning of the gendered online content that reproduces sexism and misogyny. There is also an awareness in these critiques of the young men's positionality—a self-critical stance in relation to the biases and prejudices about gender shaping theirs and others' online engagements. Ethical engagement for gender justice is further evident, as in the previous section, in the young men's concern about the negative impacts of Tate on younger boys.

Anxieties Expressing Aspects of Identity

Many of the young men spoke of the pressures they felt when representing themselves online, especially in relation to posting on social media. Such pressures related to concerns that posting stories and images was a more feminine than masculine activity, anxiety about body image standards, and comparison with peers. These pressures led to feelings of stress for many of the young men. Chen (18, G, CALD) provided insight into the emotional toll of presenting a polished online persona. He mentioned how maintaining a consistent facade of perfection in online posts can be "taxing ... like the energy and just the momentum to stay happy ... and trying to be perfect ... that you want to only pull out the best moments in your life".

Some of the young men noted that their anxiety around posting stories and images was associated with expectations to adhere to stereotypical masculine norms. Research findings on the gendered dimensions of posting, while complex, suggest that women post and edit their selfies more than men (Reed & Saunders, 2020) and that posting itself may reproduce gender stereotypes (Döring et al., 2016). Along these lines, several of the young men's comments suggested that posting (especially selfies) was, as Mateo (16, S) stated, a "more feminine [thing] to do". Relatedly, Felix (20, B) commented, "not many guys post just photos of themselves, just like looking nice or in nice clothes, which is something that most of like the female presenting people in my friend group do a lot". There seemed, in this respect, to be an othering of, or distancing from, what was viewed as the 'feminine' or female intentions of posting, as Jase (20, S, CALD) explained: "women like the attention part of the social media more than men do". Campbell (18, B, D) similarly referred to women more often than men posting for validation. For Leslie (17, S) this was about women placing more value on their online image and how they appear to others than men who tended to be far less bothered with what he inferred as quite trivial concerns: "I don't focus on making myself look good any more than 10 seconds in the mirror … like I rocked up to this interview with like bad hair and wearing [a] hoodie" (Leslie, 17, S).

In contrast to these comments, some of the young men were critical of the gendered double standards that lead women to be more concerned with their appearance and with posting for validation. Oliver (21, Q) explained:

> I think there's a lot of pressure from social media for girls, like lots of really intense standards that you can be bombarded with and then I think that sort of leads to them posting in ways that sort of show them [that they] fit that beauty standard as much as they can … a lot more pressure, I think… I probably don't feel as much because I don't think that [there] is as much of it for men, and I think it can be sad sometimes to see how overwhelming it can be and how it can really affect people's self-esteem. (Oliver, 21, Q)

These comments are consistent with other research that highlights the gendered expectations that shape how women present themselves on social media—a double bind where, on the one hand, young women receive social popularity and success for sexualised performances of femininity online but on the other hand, they receive negative judgments that such performances over-share personal experiences and are vain and attention-seeking and sexually promiscuous (Dobson, 2013; Ringrose & Barajas, 2011).

Notwithstanding these double standards, many of the young men expressed the view that posting images focusing on appearance was "anxiety-inducing" (Barry & Martin, 2016). As Åberg et al. (2020) point out, while appearance-related pressures in relation to social media sites such as Instagram and Facebook are higher for younger women, both males and females experience this pressure. For Felix (20, B) such anxiety related to the comments associated with images—he explained that men were less likely than women to receive supportive comments when they share selfies or personal photos: "it's a hell of a lot scarier when you don't know that you're actually gonna get a good reception". Tariq (19, S) noted that men expressing vulnerability through sharing stories or images tended to be met with ridicule: "we don't post publicly … it's really judgmental and especially being like a young man, putting up a vulnerable story, you're just gonna get like people laughing at you or people … criticising you". Jase (20, S, CALD) concurred that posting vulnerability can lead to negative judgments, with men being perceived as weak when sharing personal struggles.

In relation to posting and viewing others' posts, many of the young men described the negative impact of body image standards. Such negative impacts seemed to be consistent with research finding that men's body image pressures are associated with anxiety because they tend to reinforce hegemonic masculine boundaries, with power and acceptance ascribed to those who conform to an idealised masculine appearance (Barry & Martin, 2016). Ari (19, S, CALD) and Jamie (16, First Nations) shared their insecurities regarding their online experiences of body image. Ari spoke of not posting for a long time when he was younger because he didn't want people to see that he "had really bad acne". Jamie similarly spoke of avoiding posting during acne breakouts: "I didn't post because, you know, there'll be a big pimple here and I was like, yeah. I can't put that out there, that's terrible. Disgusting". Ari (19, S, CALD) noted, "on Instagram posting just feels like it has to be like perfect to post … me at my best". Consistent with the earlier discussion on fitspiration (Palmér, 2015), others described negative impacts on their body image from seeing photo and video content to do with fitness or bodybuilding. Felix (20, B) expressed "feeling bad" about unrealistic expectations of how "people should look" on social media while Hugh (20, S) noted feeling "quite bummed down" when he compared his body and gym progress with perfect "gym pictures" on social media. Kenneth (21, S) similarly mentioned feeling inferior when comparing his physique with others in gym selfies and photos posted online, while Daniel (19, G) referred to these sorts of selfies as making you feel "shit" and "self-conscious". Kieran also mentioned his physique: "I'm a very skinny small person. So, I'm not very physically masculine". He spoke of posting "a bunch of backflips" as his way of saying, 'I'm still athletic. I'm still fit". Franklin (21, S) spoke of feeling "sad" when comparing himself to others online which made him view himself "negatively", as he explained:

> like, although I consciously am aware people obviously don't post the shit parts of their lives, it's still like you're doing something which I'm not right now. You know? … the sadness I get from seeing someone do something awesome and that's me being brutally honest. (Franklin, 21, S)

Daniel (19, G) and Tyler (20, B, D) similarly noted how social media can foster a comparison-focused environment where individuals strive to showcase their achievements, as other research has documented (Laplante, 2022). This competition, as these comments suggest, can lead to self-comparisons, especially concerning major life milestones. Daniel (19, G) described posting regularly and that "there was a point in [his] life where, you know, life was kind of just like a competition and it was like, you know … you wanted to show people that you were doing these things". Tyler (20, B, D) described competitive posting as:

> …kind of a 'look at me' … [you] judge yourself … like you compare [yourself with other] people … it could be like, 'oh, yeah, look at me, like I'm doing this degree', like, you know, 'I'm having a baby' like, you know, 'I've got my life on track' that's when you compare yourself like, you know, that's not me. (Tyler, 20, B, D)

A few of the young men mentioned financial insecurity as an issue exacerbated by seeing the success their friends posted online (Laplante, 2022). Kenneth (21, S) spoke of feeling inadequate when he saw posts of his friends on holidays while he was stuck at home, while Kieran (19, S) noted how his sense of self-esteem was undermined by comparing his financial stability with his friend's:

> my biggest insecurity at the moment is money. I am broke … like if I try moving out at the moment, I would be moving out for a piece of cardboard so that's probably, you know, when I see … friends, my age or younger than me moving out and actually, you know, being able to get jobs … that's probably the biggest thing that I see online is for the, you know, look at … where I am. (Kieran, 19, S)

It is evident that people tend to present a positive version of themselves on social media (Laplante, 2022) and that the social comparisons that result can lead to social anxiety and undermine self-esteem (Jiang & Ngien, 2020). Along these lines, Maxie (21, S, CALD) and Brodie (20, B) highlighted the unhealthy aspect of comparing their lives to others' online representations. Maxie commented, "Yeah, I know some people who literally attend events just for that one good picture … like people always wanna show up the good parts of their life but it's unhealthy to compare it to other people." Brodie (20, B) referred to the internet as "just like a competitive game for like the best pictures, the best videos like, you know, looking the best and all that sort of thing". Similarly, Mike (20, S) and Geoffrey (20, G, CALD) noted how social media platforms encourage individuals to present idealised versions of themselves, which can contribute to a lack of authenticity in online interactions. As Mike (20, S) commented, “when you travel yourself, there’s obviously some amazing bits, but … there’s a lot of lower points” that people don’t post. Geoffrey (20, G, CALD) added, “I think everyone’s trying to look a certain way and everyone’s projecting something on to the internet, otherwise people wouldn’t be on the internet.”

As a way to present themselves in the best possible way and manage comparison anxiety (Jiang & Ngien, 2020), a few of the young men reflected on the curated performance of posting online. They highlighted the effort that goes into crafting an online image. Jacob (21, S) stated, “most of the people in my [friendship group] a lot of effort goes into deciding what you’re putting up there or like, how you present yourself for your image” while Benito (20, S, CALD) commented, “a hundred percent with Instagram … people plan out specifically where they’re going to post at a certain time”.

The comments in this section, in a similar way to the previous section, reflect struggles with what constitutes an ethical engagement with expressing aspects of identity online. These struggles relate to what the young men believe to be good and important for themselves particularly in relation to alleviating their anxieties and the emotional toll of their online engagements. The young men’s reluctance to post and express vulnerability online indicates that they are accepting responsibility and accountability (in terms of managing their anxieties). However, as noted earlier, this is problematic because it frames ethical engagement as a personal responsibility rather than the responsibility of online platforms.

These ethical struggles informed the young men’s curatorial intentionality—evident in their absence of posting and their efforts to craft a curated online identity. They exercise agency by selectively presenting or not presenting aspects of themselves (again, this is accepted as a personal responsibility). Some of this curation affirms rigid gender norms—e.g., some young men avoid posting selfies, associating this act with an inferior femininity - while other aspects of curatorial intentionality challenge these norms. The latter are visible in the young men’s recognition of the gendered double standards shaping different posting practices between women and men and of the pressures shaping young men’s reluctance to post (i.e., masculinity as invulnerable) or to post images that conform to unrealistic masculine body and life standards.

The Affordances and Harms of Online Anonymity

Online anonymity offers both affordances and harms for young men. It enables authentic self-expression, circumvention of social norms, self-exploration and the development of relationships (Ellison et al., 2016; Keipi & Oksanen, 2014). Online anonymity can also be harmful in the form of cyberbullying and harassment (Keipi, 2018).

Several of the young men noted that the anonymity of online spaces supported freedom of expression (Pangrazio, 2018). As Brendan (20, S) explained, anonymity allows "people to express themselves" in ways "that they normally wouldn't". He added:

> when you're anonymous on the internet ... you don't need to worry about embarrassing yourself ... you can kind of take on a character that you wouldn't normally take, experiment a bit, like say something you probably wouldn't normally say [or] act a certain way ... whereas in person, everyone's a little bit more [reserved] you know, keep to yourself a bit more, a little bit, just worry about that kind of stuff ... [Online] if you [are] embarrassed, you'll just leave the server and do another one. (Brendan, 20, S)

Campbell (18, B, D) similarly found that the anonymity offered by sites like Reddit allowed him to "just like lurk in there and post stuff that you usually wouldn't on other social media without ... judgment of others ... I feel like [you] can be more open and like experiment with stuff online". For Danveer (18, S, CALD), the anonymity of some online spaces was positive because it enabled him to express and share "deep stuff" about himself that he felt he couldn't share with friends and that this relieved his stress:

> I don't find it embarrassing ... like you're not gonna meet them ever, you know ... you're just gonna be on a call with them ... or on text as well ... None of your friends are gonna know so like if you tell them deep stuff, it relieves yourself like it relieves your feelings, like relieves the stress in simplest words ...like you can say anything you want to them [and] if they tell others, it doesn't matter, 'cause you don't even know them. And it's not gonna come back up to you again. (Danveer, 18, S, CALD)

In these comments a sense of perceived authenticity is evident in the young men's use of anonymity to express themselves freely without fear of embarrassment or judgment (Ellison et al., 2016). For Brendan (20, S) and Campbell (18, B, D), anonymity enables them to experiment with self-expression and engage in conversations they might avoid in face-to-face interactions, while Danveer (18, S, CALD) finds relief in sharing "deep stuff" anonymously, which helped alleviate his stress. Here anonymity fosters a sense of authenticity by removing the pressure of maintaining a socially acceptable persona (Ellison et al., 2016).

Several of the young men spoke of creating fake accounts to take advantage of the affordances of anonymity in ways that supported a flexible approach to identity management and self-representation (Ellison et al., 2016). Warren (18, S), for example, mentioned using second non-identifiable Snapchat and Instagram accounts for security reasons to keep a distance from new people he had just met and did not trust yet. Others commented positively on the visual anonymity online spaces afforded, utilising anonymity for initiating and developing relationships (Ellison et al., 2016). Miles (16, S), for example, mentioned the opportunity to make friends with people irrespective of their perceived level of attractiveness:

> It's easy to talk to people online than it is to talk to them face to face. And then obviously [it's] easier to make friends with them. ... Maybe [in real life, people] don't wanna be friends with someone who isn't like, the nicest looking. Whereas just in text, that's not like something you can see. (Miles 16, S)

Some of the young men recognised the harms of online anonymity, particularly how harassment and other negative behaviours can be enabled by anonymity (Keipi, 2018). Lionel (20, S), for example, outlined his experiences of hostility online, stating his view that online environments made it easier to treat others poorly: "I mean, there's a lot of arseholes in real life and everyone can access the internet ... yeah, people are definitely more comfortable with being arseholes to other people online if no one knows who they are." For Jin (19, S, CALD), gaming environments were enabling of hostility that people would otherwise not express. He explained that there were:

> specific games where people hop on and they're a completely different version of themselves where they like flame [insult or attack] people and like be super, get super upset ... [the] game is just like an out for them. (Jin, 19, S, CALD)

Simon (19, Ax) considered anonymity as enabling "people [to] get away with what they want because [their anonymity] protects them … [and it's] like running straight into a brick wall trying to find out who they are." Similarly, Leslie (17, S) found that anonymity allows users to "just hide behind their screens, you know, because in one click of a button, they can just be gone from that so, you can yeah, [be] a lot more cocky and like not yourself behind your screen, because you don't really face any consequence for it". For Chen (18, G, CALD) a lack of account verification allowed people to spread hate:

> Because of social media people can create accounts where they don't have any actual personal information tied to them so because of that, they can really just kind of spew a lot of hate. Yes, just like negative comments … [saying things] like, oh, they're ugly, [they're] shit … very attacking. (Chen, 18, G, CALD)

Some of the young men admitted to using their anonymity online to engage in these negative sorts of behaviours—to troll (posting deliberately offensive or provocative content), mess with and torment other users. Ned (17, S, CALD) explained his engagement in "a bit of trolling" about "soccer opinions" and "favourite players" on Twitter (X) and Instagram with the purpose of getting "diehard fans" "angry", to "get a bit of a laugh out of it." "It's pretty funny to get them upset," he added. Miles (16, S) spoke of using an old Discord account to "lightly mess with people, just for fun", while Omer (17, S, CALD) considered it normal for people to have alternate anonymous accounts to "torment" people.

The use of anonymity by the young men sometimes wandered into questionable ethical territory. Mateo (16, S), for example, participated in what is known as online vigilantism with a friend to target older men by pretending to be underage girls:

> I've, I've got a story, like, me and my mates, we, we made these accounts, and we pretended to be like 13-year-old girls, and we joined these groups with like 50-year-old men. I talk to them acting like this, you know, it goes and they like, crazy, man … most of [the photos they sent] was like a shirtless pic … I didn't ask but they just sent it. And others were more, you know, special photos. We're gonna, we're gonna like, screen share and then like find them on Facebook and then find his wife and like, send it to her. (Mateo, 16, S)

Alistair (16, B, D) talked in similar terms about anonymity online and, more specifically, how his use of a different female-sounding name on his Instagram attracted messages from older men who presumed he was female. He explained, "on that one platform, they do definitely talk to me differently as if I'm a girl, cause it's not like a video call, it's just messages". Kieran (19, S) expressed concern about the ease with which individuals can disguise themselves online and engage in harmful behaviours, especially in interactions involving vulnerable individuals, such as children, as he explained: "there's people that can do quite a bit of harm to someone who's on there, who doesn't know what they're doing" or with whom they are communicating. He emphasised the potential dangers, such as online predators targeting young users, highlighting the challenge of identifying such threats compared to real-world situations where suspicious behaviour is more readily noticeable.

The young men's critical digital dispositions are evident in this section in their curatorial intentionality, particularly their strategic use of anonymity to explore identities, share emotions, and participate in online communities without fear of judgment. As with the previous sections, it seems that the young men's ethical struggles with anonymity inform this curation—what they consider as good and important are online spaces where they feel free to express themselves and experiment without being judged. However, for some of the young men such expression is not mindful of what is good and important for others, e.g., Danver's comment: "you can say anything … it doesn't matter, 'cause you don't even know them". For others, however, there was recognition of the harms perpetrated by such anonymity. Here ethical engagements considered the risks and harms associated with anonymity, such as enabling harassment and unethical behaviours. The young men's use of anonymity for trolling and vigilantism compromises ethical engagement. As with some of the earlier observations, such use bypasses accountability and ignores the impacts of actions such as trolling on others.

Conclusion

This chapter has highlighted the contradictory ways young men experience leisure, work, and identity online. On the one hand, digital spaces provide entertainment, connection, and self-improvement, but on the other hand, they generate anxieties about overuse, body image, and self-presentation. The analysis highlighted moments of curatorial intentionality, scepticism, ethical engagement, and reflexivity, while also revealing the young men's tendency to internalise responsibility for managing digital harms – an individualisation that shifts accountability away from the systemic and structural forces that create and sustain these harms. The following chapter explores the young men's experiences of connection, community and conflict in online spaces.

References

Åberg, E., Koivula, A., & Kukkonen, I. (2020). A feminine burden of perfection? Appearance-related pressures on social networking sites. *Telematics and Informatics, 46*, 101319.

Adorjan, M., & Ricciardelli, R. (2021). Smartphone and social media addiction: Exploring the perceptions and experiences of Canadian teenagers. *Canadian Review of Sociology/Revue canadienne de sociologie, 58*(1), 45–64.

Barry, B., & Martin, D. (2016). Fashionably fit: Young men's dress decisions and appearance anxieties. *Textile, 14*(3), 326–347.

Dobson, A. (2013). Laddishness online: The possible significations and significance of 'performative shamelessness' for young women in the post-feminist context. *Cultural Studies, 28*(1), 142–164.

Dontre, A. J. (2020). The influence of technology on academic distraction: A review. *Human Behavior and Emerging Technologies, 3*(3), 379–390. https://doi.org/10.1002/hbe2.229

Döring, N., Reif, A., & Poeschl, S. (2016). How gender-stereotypical are selfies? A content analysis and comparison with magazine adverts. *Computers in Human Behavior, 55*, 955–962.

Dyer, H. T. (2015). All the web's a stage: The effects of design and modality on youth performances of identity. In *Technology and youth: Growing up in a digital world* (Sociological studies of children and youth) (Vol. 19, pp. 213–242). https://doi.org/10.1108/S1537-466120150000019007

Ellison, N. B., Blackwell, L., Lampe, C., & Trieu, P. (2016). "The question exists, but you don't exist with it": Strategic anonymity in the social lives of adolescents. *Social Media + Society, 2*(4), 205630511667067. https://doi.org/10.1177/2056305116670673

eSafety Commissioner. (2018). *State of play: Youth, kids and digital dangers*. https://www.esafety.gov.au/sites/default/files/2019-10/State%20of%20Play%20-%20Youth%20kids%20and%20digital%20dangers.pdf

eSafety Commissioner. (2021). *The digital lives of Aussie teens*. https://www.esafety.gov.au/sites/default/files/2021-02/The%20digital%20lives%20of%20Aussie%20teens.pdf?v=1739413907704 eSafety Commissioner. (2024). *Being a young man online: Tensions, complexities and possibilities*. https://www.esafety.gov.au/sites/default/files/2024-06/Being-a-young-man-online-June-2024.pdf?v=1739413767503

Feltham, F. (2024). I'm Andrew Tate's audience and I know why he appeals to young men. *The Guardian*. https://www.theguardian.com/news/2024/jan/06/im-andrew-tates-audience-and-i-know-why-he-appeals-to-young-men

Hefner, D., Knop, K., & Vorderer, P. (2018). "I wanna be in the loop!"—The role of fear of missing out (FoMO) for the quantity and quality of young adolescents' mobile phone use: Current perspectives on media use and effects. In R. Kühne, S. E. Baumgartner, T. Koch, & M. Hofer (Eds.), *Youth and media: Current perspectives on media use and effects* (1st ed., pp. 39–54). Nomos Verlagsgesellschaft mbH & Co. KG.

Jiang, S., & Ngien, A. (2020). The effects of Instagram use, social comparison, and self-esteem on social anxiety: A survey study in Singapore. *Social Media + Society, 6*(2), 2056305120912488.

Keddie, A., Roose, J., & Flood, M. (2024). 'I don't really wanna consume his content': What do young Australian men think of Andrew Tate? *The Conversation*. https://theconversation.com/i-dont-really-wanna-consume-his-content-what-do-young-australian-men-think-of-andrew-tate-233654

Keipi, T. (2018). Relatedness online: An analysis of youth narratives concerning the effects of internet anonymity. *Young, 26*(2), 91–107. https://doi.org/10.1177/1103308817715142

Keipi, T., & Oksanen, A. (2014). Self-exploration, anonymity and risks in the online setting: Analysis of narratives by 14–18-year olds. *Journal of Youth Studies, 17*(8), 1097–1113.

Laplante, S. (2022) How social media can crush your self-esteem, The Conversation, available at: https://theconversation.com/how-social-media-can-crush-your-self-esteem-174009

Palmér, L. (2015). "Poppin' bottles, getting wheysted." Exploring young men's engagement with fitspiration content and its consequential influences on attitudes and behaviour. *Journal of Promotional Communications, 3*, 425–445.

Pangrazio, L. (2018). *Young people's literacies in the digital age: Continuities, conflicts and contradictions*. Routledge.

Potter, J. (2012). *Digital media and learner identity*. Palgrave Macmillan.

Reed, P., & Saunders, J. (2020). Sex differences in online assertive self-presentation strategies. *Personality and Individual Differences, 166*, 110214. https://doi.org/10.1016/j.paid.2020.110214

Ringrose, J., & Barajas, K. (2011). Gendered risks and opportunities? Exploring teen girls' digitized sexual identities in postfeminist media contexts. *International Journal of Media & Cultural Politics, 7*(2), 121–138.

Roberts, S., Jones, C., Nicholas, L., Wescott, S., & Maloney, M. (2025). Beyond the clickbait: Analysing the masculinist ideology in Andrew Tate's online written discourses. *Cultural Sociology*. https://doi.org/10.1177/17499755241307414

Samari, E., Chang, S., Seow, E., Chua, Y. C., Subramaniam, M., van Dam, R. M., Luo, N., Verma, S., & Vaingankar, J. A. (2022). A qualitative study on negative experiences of social media use and harm reduction strategies among youths in a multi-ethnic Asian society. *PLoS ONE, 17*(11). https://doi.org/10.1371/journal.pone.0277928

Santos-Meneses, L. F. (2021). Thinking critically through controversial issues on digital media: Dispositions and key criteria for content evaluation. *Thinking Skills and Creativity, 42*, 100927. https://doi.org/10.1016/j.tsc.2021.100927

Stenalt, M. H. (2021). Digital student agency: Approaching agency in digital contexts from a critical perspective. *Frontline Learning Research, 9*(3), 52–68. https://doi.org/10.14786/flr.v9i3.697

The Man Cave. (2023). Who is Andrew Tate and why do young men relate to him. https://themancave.life/andrew-tate-report/

Thompson, D. (2025). The anti-social century. *The Atlantic*. https://www.theatlantic.com/magazine/archive/2025/02/american-loneliness-personality-politics/681091/

CHAPTER 3

Connection, Community and Conflict

Abstract In this chapter the focus is on connection, community and conflict. It explores how the young men derive a sense of belonging, acceptance and support through social media and gaming experiences. Whether expressed through a desire for acceptance in friendship groups, the refuge found in safe online spaces, or the positive feelings of inclusion in specific online communities, an overarching theme is a pursuit of connection free from judgment. These same spaces and communities, however, can also be harmful and abusive. They can foster negativity and hostility, ranging from transphobia to online hate and competitive "trash-talk". These negative experiences prompt some of the young men to disengage and opt out. The young men's critical engagement in these spaces extends beyond the content they encounter to the architecture of specific online platforms, such as Twitter (X), which are recognised as promoting polarisation and hostility. The chapter provides analytic summaries throughout to highlight how the young men are engaging with curatorial intentionality, scepticism, ethical engagement and reflexivity [Pangrazio, L. (2018). *Young people's literacies in the digital age: Continuities, conflicts and contradictions.* Routledge].

Keywords Young men • Connection • Community • Conflict • Online engagements • Social media • Gaming

A. Keddie, M. Flood, *Young Men's Online Lives*,
https://doi.org/10.1007/978-3-031-99980-2_3

Online Communities as Connection, Belonging and Acceptance

Connecting with friends, family and community was central to the online experiences of the young men in this study. Such connections led to the young men feeling a sense of belonging and acceptance. Other research, too, has found that for young men or young people more generally, social media platforms and online gaming communities provide invaluable opportunities for social connection (Davis, 2012; Fu, 2018; Pietersen et al., 2019). Digital spaces allow for flexible interactions and can foster a sense of belonging among geographically dispersed individuals (Dørum et al., 2010; Peacock et al., 2020; Brodie & Osowska, 2021). As noted in the previous chapter, young men drew on a range of different applications and platforms for connecting with friends, family and community. Most of the young men used platforms such as Snapchat and Instagram for connecting with their friends and Facebook and to a lesser extent WhatsApp (including group chats) for connecting with family. Facebook was named as a popular platform for connecting with older friends and for university studies and was also used to connect to broader communities, as were apps like Discord.

Online apps and platforms played an important role in sustaining not only the young men's family relationships but their friendships. As Dev (19, S, CALD) and Julian (19, S, CALD), explained, "I've been able to reconnect with friends, like really old friends who I've lost touch with" (Dev, 19, S, CALD); "being online, actually allowed me to reconnect with some of the people from my school that I didn't talk to for a while … that was a pretty positive experience online" (Julian (19, S, CALD).

Many of the young men shared their experiences of feeling connected through common interest groups on apps such as Facebook and Discord. Felix (20, B), for example, reported that a "mountaineering club at [his] university through Facebook messenger led to a lot of really really cool experiences and trips over the past two, three months". Kieran (19, S) noted his positive experiences within specialised Facebook groups related to shared interests, such as a group focused on costuming in the space Western television series The Mandalorian: "[it's] just awesome … that sort of community, everyone there really enjoys that and everyone [is] there to help out … a really big sense of community and that's probably the most positive". Jase (20, S, CALD) and Vish (20, S, CALD) mentioned how Discord serves as a hub for activity groups and clubs - they appreciated the camaraderie that was formed based on shared interests.

Many of the young men commented on the sense of belonging they experienced in being members of online groups. Eugene (19, S), for example, expressed a deep desire for acceptance and feeling valued within his friendship group online, as he explained: "I really yearn for that feeling of acceptance, my big thing is just feeling like I belong in a group, like in a friend group". Toby (16, S) emphasised the positive impact of being accepted into specific online groups, such as group chats or forums, as fostering a sense of belonging and purpose, free from judgment:

> things that make [social media] really positive for me is that if I'm accepted by a group, like a specific group chat, I would feel really good … and then you kind of feel accepted because that's like, you know, your group of people … just there's no judgment, you know, you're into the same things, you feel like you kind of have a purpose. (Toby, 16, S)

These findings also show some similarities with research among older adults, documenting that computer-mediated communication facilitates feelings of belonging and provides opportunities for reciprocal support (Fuss et al., 2021). Online experiences of interaction, connection and community can contribute to improved well-being, reduced anxiety, and increased enjoyment in educational settings (Archard, 2014; Brodie & Osowska, 2021; Peacock et al., 2020) and may have similar impacts elsewhere.

For young gay, bisexual, queer, and trans men, queer spaces online may be particularly important in fostering self-acceptance and a sense of community belonging. Oliver (21, Q) commented on his connection to an online LGBTQI+ community on TikTok as positive—it was a context where he could "feel a lot more normal which can be good especially when like you're not surrounded by that". Similarly, Trevor (17, B, D) highlighted the importance of safe spaces in creating a positive online environment for him, as he explained:

> For me, it's more about feeling safe and accepted. So, yeah, honestly, just places that aren't really fuelled with as much hate, like it can be like as simple as some video, someone saying, oh yeah, good night everyone, like just things that feel like no matter who you are, you're accepted and cared about in that moment. (Trevor, 17, B, D)

For Daniel (19, G), social media helped him connect with the LGBTQI+ community and explore shared interests, as he explained:

> I identify as gay so I kind of find that easier to connect with the community that I am also in, you know, there's a big gay community that's in Sydney, so it kind of helps you keep that connection to them at the same time, especially through Instagram. (Daniel, 19, G)

Similarly, other research has found that for LGBTQI+ youth, platforms such as Tumblr offer spaces to explore identity and connect with others (Byron et al., 2019). Queer sites can provide a sense of community, lessen isolation, connect LGBTQI+ youth to resources and networks, and enable political participation (Hanckel & Morris, 2014).

A few of the young men noted that their online social connections meant being able to reach out, "when you're going through some stuff, it's always nice having, you know, knowing these people [are] around and knowing you have those connections … so you've always got people you can talk to straight away". Ren (19, S, CALD) described the significance of "hav[ing] meaningful conversations… sometimes, like, you know, you might need some help, but can't be with everyone together" while Finn (16, S, CALD) commented on the "nice communit[ies]" he belonged to "where [there are people you] can talk to" as well as "being supportive when something goes wrong".

Online gaming was mentioned as a way that some young men connected with friends and fostered new connections, and this is evident in other research as well (Weinstein & James, 2022). Nathan (17, S), for example, spoke of the significance of online gaming in his life: "I play games quite a lot with my friends, it's really our primary means of like doing things together because none of us really particularly likes hanging out physically, we prefer to just play games together." Ari (19, S, CALD) mentioned multiplayer games such as Fortnite, League of Legends, Rainbow Six Siege, and Overwatch as fostering connections. He shared an anecdote about his group of friends collectively exploring the challenging game Hollow Knight. Quinn (20, S) similarly noted his enjoyment in gaming, often playing popular titles like Fortnite, Rocket League, and Apex Legends with his friends. These multiplayer and single-player games offer not just entertainment but also opportunities for bonding and shared experiences. Several of the young men noted using Discord to connect with community. Ari (19, S, CALD) spoke of Discord as a popular platform for gamers. He mentioned being part of a server with around 60 friends who regularly engage in voice chats, playing games together and enjoying each other's company. Derek (20, S, CALD) discussed his involvement in a Formula One (car racing) group, noting the sense of camaraderie within these large digital gatherings.

The comments in this section highlight the centrality of online communities in supporting young men's sense of connection, belonging, and acceptance. Whether expressed through the desire for acceptance in friendship groups, the refuge found in safe spaces, or the positive feelings of inclusion in specific online communities, an overarching theme is a pursuit of connection free from judgment. These connections serve as avenues for building relations and gaining support—in ways that are not limited by physical boundaries (Weinstein & James, 2022).

The young men's comments offer a nuanced exploration of the gendered dimensions within their pursuit of acceptance, belonging, and emotional support in online communities. Traditionally, societal expectations of masculinity often uphold stoicism, emotional detachment, and an aversion to vulnerability. However, the experiences recounted here challenge these conventional norms. Acts of reconnecting with old friends and maintaining relationships with family members reflect a desire for emotional closeness and a willingness to express affection. The shared experiences within common interest groups further challenge traditional gender norms where ideal masculinities are associated with competitive individualism. Whether participating in a mountaineering club, a TV series costuming group, or an LGBTQI+ community, the young men express a need for social acceptance and emotional connections (Keddie & Bartel, 2021). The young men's valuing of online communities as sources of support during difficult times further challenges the masculine ideal of self-reliance and highlights the importance placed on seeking help and finding comfort within social networks. Rather than providing only shallow interpersonal ties (Twenge, 2013), online communities for these young men are a means of connection, belonging and acceptance.

In this section, the young men's critical digital dispositions are evident in their curatorial intentionality, as they strategically select platforms such as Instagram, Snapchat, Discord and Facebook to maintain relationships and align their digital activities with personal and social interests (Pangrazio, 2018). While this curation is not entirely neutral—i.e., algorithmic structures and digital architectures influence their accessibility and engagement, often steering them toward male-dominated spaces like gaming servers or specialised Discord groups—the young men are agentic in their navigation of these spaces to align with their preferences. As with the previous chapter, this curatorial intentionality is shaped by a sense of ethical engagement and reflexivity. The young men acknowledge the impact of digital spaces on their emotional and social well-being—their strong desire for connection and belonging reflects what they conceptualise as important and good for themselves and others and they express a sense of responsibility to maintain online communities that are safe, inclusive and respectful.

Online Communities as Harmful and Abusive

Online communities were also spaces of abuse and harm for many of the young men in this research. For Simon (19, Ax), negativity online was to be expected and something that required conscious detachment:

> I understand that there's a lot of negativity online, but I mean, that's to be expected, but everywhere you go, people are gonna be dicks. Yeah, it doesn't affect me much. I just let it be and I can't change them, so why should I try? (Simon, 19, Ax)

Geoffrey (20, G, CALD) aligned the harm and abuse prevalent in online communities with the phenomenon of people feeling entitled to comment on various issues even when those issues do not directly affect them:

> I feel like social media has given people an idea that they have a right and the need to commentate on everything, like trans people. I think it's a perfect issue because you've got people who [have] never met a trans person and, you know, they're just piling on and going on with absolute bullshit and it's frankly, it doesn't even make sense to me like at the first point, like why you feel you need to comment on something that doesn't even affect you at all? (Geoffrey, 20, G, CALD)

Dylan (18, S, CALD) reflected on how online platforms like X (formerly Twitter) have changed over time, from being "welcoming" to "deteriorating in recent years" due to increased arguments. Henry (16, S) echoed Dylan's sentiments regarding X, noting how what used to be a space "to safely share your opinions" had now become a negative space for arguments and being "attacked for [what] you are saying". Maverick (19, Prefer not to say) referred to Reddit as a platform that allows users to explore popular posts worldwide, but that this often means exposure to a significant amount of negativity and hate in the comments sections. He expressed his aversion to such negativity, attributing it to a sense of "misguided hate" and "ignorance". Maverick also pointed out that the platform's design tends to amplify negative content because people are more likely to engage with it when they are upset or passionate about a particular issue. This amplification of negativity, he noted, can overshadow positive content.

These young men's encounters with negativity and hate online are unsurprising, given that abuse, harassment, and hate speech are well-documented phenomena in online spaces (Castaño-Pulgarín et al., 2021). For example, hate speech—bias-motivated, hostile, and malicious language targeted at a person or group because of their actual or perceived innate characteristics—is prevalent not only on hate groups' websites and forums but in general online discussion across a variety of popular platforms (Siegel, 2020). Although hate speech is only a small proportion of the speech e.g. on Twitter (Siegel et al., 2019), large numbers of people have been exposed incidentally to online hate speech, such as 53% of Americans among users aged 15–30 (Siegel, 2020).

Jamie (16, First Nations) also mentioned the potential harm of platforms including Twitter (X) and Reddit that delve into dark and personal subjects. He noted that in engaging with such communities, individuals with similar struggles can inadvertently reinforce negative behaviours and attitudes. In his view the internet is an enabling space for self-harm because people are able to interact with "so many people who have the same feelings … [all] banding together in a negative way". Relatedly, Toby (16, S) shared an example from a Discord server focused on mental health that he engaged with as a support person who tried to give "advice" and "help out". He described encountering numerous messages from individuals self-harming and "venting" about "how depressed they" are. Toby described the toll it took on him being in this space and feeling that he was not able to help the people in this group.

In coping with these harms, many of the young men spoke of removing themselves from these platforms and spaces. Maverick (19, Prefer not to say) spoke of staying away from negative online spaces. Jesse (18, S) also mentioned how he was "tired" of seeing "really "negative" and "upsetting" things online and that this led to him having to "take a break every once in a while from the internet". Trevor (17, B, D), a trans man, mentioned "how uncomfortable" he felt on the internet sometimes with people debating his identity—a transphobia that proposed that trans men should change what he described as "fundamentally impossible things to change about [himself]". He described this as "distressing" and as prompting him to take a break from online activities.

Vincent (21, S) highlighted the ease of getting caught up in negative online discussions and noted the presence of racism and sexism in online contexts. He spoke of choosing not to engage in these threads, recognising that they rarely lead to productive or positive outcomes. Jaden (19, G, CALD), in contrast, reported having a high threshold for offence and suggested that individuals who dislike certain content should simply avoid it—"if you don't like it, don't look at it". Racist, transphobic, and other antagonistic content may be particularly troubling for young men who are members of the targeted groups, as well as those who are more politically liberal, as other research finds (Siegel, 2020).

Some young men in this research identified dynamics that amplify online hostilities. Christian (17, S, D) and Kyle (18, S, CALD) discussed the phenomenon of 'band wagoning' as prevalent in online spaces, where enthusiastic individuals come together to express often negative and polarising views, amplifying one another's sentiments. For Kyle (18, S, CALD), the Andrew Tate phenomena was a case in point, as he explained: "I mean a good example of [band wagoning] is probably, you know, Andrew Tate, a lot of people, all of their opinions about him are probably formed by, you know, what other people think". Mateo (16, S) similarly spoke about the influence of social media, highlighting how easy it is for opinions and perceptions to be swayed by online interactions. Ulysses (G18) described internet culture as "mean-spirited", adding that "most of the stuff nowadays is just kind of 'I'm gonna make fun of you' yeah, it's just not great".

Gaming cultures were mentioned by many of the young men as communities where toxicity, verbal abuse and competition were prevalent. This is consistent with research in this space (Massanari, 2017; Braithwaite, 2016). Studies have found a high prevalence of harassment, with 66% of gamers experiencing toxic behaviours in the past year (Zsila et al., 2022). Common forms of harmful behaviour include verbal abuse, gender-based harassment, and sexual innuendos (Maharani et al., 2024). These behaviours negatively impact players' wellbeing, enjoyment, gaming retention, and mental health (Beres et al., 2021; Zsila et al., 2022).

Many of these patterns were evident in young men's experience in this research. Eugene (19, S), for example, named specific multiplayer competitive games such as League of Legends "as notoriously toxic". He explained, "I think everyone's a little bit exaggerated ... everyone's a little over passionate about wanting to win". He mentioned how the competitive nature of these games can lead to frustrations and verbal abuse among players, especially if you have to "make up for the mistakes of teammates ... it's infuriating at times". Eugene mentioned that when he was younger, he was "banned as a result" of verbal abuse. Bairam (18, S, CALD) also mentioned being "banned" from a game for an "entire week" when he was about 15 years old for saying things he "wouldn't normally say".

Ari (19, S, CALD) similarly described the challenges of dealing with toxic teammates who send racial slurs and death threats during games, as he explained:

> people will like [trash-talk] like as close to the N-word as possible without actually like breaching the game's terms of services ... you can just tell that this player is going to be ... abusive, toxic, whatever. It's something I'm unfortunately used to playing a lot of competitive online games. (Ari, 19, S, CALD)

Others mentioned the explicit and derogatory language used in online gaming. Omer (17, S, CALD) stated "it's actually how I discovered a bunch of slurs that I didn't know existed"; Mateo (16, S) said "that's how you find half the swear words"; Stephen (16, S) noted "you get 12-year-olds calling you the N-word"; and Scott (16, S) reported "I got my account permanently banned [because] I was a bit too toxic".

Trash-talking as a common aspect of gaming culture was also noted by Franklin (21, S). He attributed it to the competitive nature of gaming and the predominantly young male player base: "I think it's because the gaming community is predominantly young males ... it is very competitive, and sometimes you let out that frustration through hurtful comments". Scott (16, S) agreed: "I would say that they're like, it's a very like male dominated thing I would say that's why it's racist and sexist as well." Trevor (17, B, D) also noted his experience of gender-based harassment given he "sounded a lot more feminine [when he was younger] because [his] voice hadn't dropped yet". He described copping "a whole bunch of shit just for [sounding] like a girl" which prompted him to play "non-voice chat games" to escape abuse.

Maxie (21, S, CALD) pointed out that online gaming environments often lack "repercussions for saying what you say", leading to increased toxicity. He mentioned that he had contributed to this toxic culture when he was on "the receiving end" of trash-talk and noted that ego can also play a role, with players using trash-talk as a way to assert themselves in the game: "people start talking shit about you, your ego gets hurt, you wanna [get] some kind of high ground on them and that's when all that kind of stuff just happens".

Factors contributing to toxicity in gaming cultures, according to the literature, include younger age, male gender, high achievement motivation, impulsivity, and emotional reactivity (Lemercier-Dugarin et al., 2021). Younger players and those who spend more time gaming are at higher risk of victimisation (Zsila et al., 2022). Competitive games, especially multiplayer online battle arena games and shooting games, are more prone to toxic incidents (Zsila et al., 2022).

Other young men mentioned the harmful dimensions of competitive online gaming but were less concerned about them. Devon (21, S), for example, expressed the view that "you kind of go in with the assumption that people are gonna be aggressive and you kind of just match it immediately." Mack (19, U, CALD) commented, "I don't know who this person was, but he was really bashing me hard but, I think, yeah, over time, it kind of was like, I didn't really take it personally". Brendan (20, S) commented:

> people hopping on the mic just say some pretty crazy stuff ... it's just part of being in the space ... like it's bad but like when people [are] online, they just say whatever the fuck they want, like they, you know, like, they probably didn't even mean half the shit they're saying, [they're] just trying to get a reaction ... like, you know, [I] don't think too much about it ... it washes off you. I suppose you're gonna be a little bit used to [it] as well. If you're gonna get upset over like everything people say, you know, it's like you're gonna be upset all the time, right? 'Cause there's always people saying stuff that's gonna make you upset. (Brendan, 20, S)

Henry (16, S) and Cedric (18, S) viewed trash-talk in competitive games as just part of the deal: "everyone else is doing it and [you] have to retaliate" (Henry, 16, S). They suggested that most players understand it is all in good fun and rarely taken seriously: "there's definitely a lot of trash-talk but everyone yeah, everyone knows it's not serious"

(Cedric, 18, S). This reflects other research in gaming which finds that young men describe trash-talking as a form of fun or entertainment, a way to bond with friends and teammates, and a legitimate way to gain a competitive edge when directed at opponents (Kaye et al., 2022). On the other hand, trash-talking is seen as less acceptable and as straying into illegitimate aggression or bullying if it takes place off the 'field', is directed at a person's intimate others, or takes place in inappropriate game genres such as cooperative and creative games (Kaye et al., 2022). However, some players normalise toxicity as an acceptable part of competitive gaming (Beres et al., 2021; Adinolf & Türkay, 2018).

Kristian (21, S, CALD) similarly noted how the prevalence of trash-talk in competitive online gaming communities meant that he had become "completely desensitised to it … when it happens, no surprise". He pointed out however, that his "competitive streak" in these games had:

> very much tempered over the years. … I think over the years I've kind of just lost that kind of desire to be, you know, like the absolute best when I'm playing an online video game and it's [now] much more around the social aspect and enjoyment … [when I was younger and frustrated] … then, I was like, definitely a low point [when I punched the monitor] … and then I was like, oh, what am I doing? I actually like punched a monitor because of this video game that I lost.

Juxtaposed against the comments in the previous section, these remarks highlight the paradoxical nature of online communities—they are spaces of connection and acceptance but also harm and abuse. These remarks illustrate how many young men grapple with the pervasive negativity and hostility of online spaces, prompting some to disengage and opt out of these spaces. It is heartening to see a critique not only of the negative content young men engage with online (e.g., transphobia) but also of the ways in which the architecture of particular online spaces such as Twitter (X) encourages polarisation, negativity and hostility (Pangrazio, 2018). As Light (2013) argues, the different affordances of social media platforms produce different forms of relationships and different identities and practices—some offer space to interrogate traditional masculinities while others do not.

Harm and abuse are particularly prevalent within male-dominated gaming spaces (Braithwaite, 2016; Massanari, 2017). Gaming cultures often amplify and reinforce stereotypical ideals of masculinity that valorise competition, dominance, and unchecked aggression (Geena Davis Institute et al., 2021). Racial slurs, homophobia, sexism and other harmful "trash-talk" seem to be a taken-for-granted and normalised part of gaming, with a lack of repercussions for this behaviour appearing to escalate its prevalence and severity (Braithwaite, 2016). Normalised trash-talk and abuse seem also to have desensitised some of these young men who expect to receive and contribute to aggressive gaming climates with their own trash-talk. These 'networked masculinities' within male-dominated gaming spaces co-produce and reproduce problematic norms of masculinity (Light, 2013; Braithwaite, 2016).

In this section, the young men's critical digital dispositions are evident in how they manage their engagement with online communities, particularly in avoiding spaces they perceive as excessively negative or hostile (curatorial intentionality). Many discuss deliberately stepping away from 'toxic' platforms to avoid harmful discussions, reflecting a strategic approach to protecting their well-being. However, these efforts are often challenged by platform structures that amplify negative interactions through algorithmic design. Platforms like Reddit, Twitter (X), and Discord encourage engagement with controversial content, making it difficult for users to fully disengage. While some of the young men effectively curate their digital environments to reduce harm, others find themselves drawn into this harm, exposing the limitations of individual control over digital experiences.

The young men also demonstrate scepticism in their awareness of online hostility and the performative nature of digital debates. Many recognise how gaming communities and platforms incentivise polarisation, outrage, and reactionary content, fostering cycles of negativity. Reflexivity and a desire for a more ethical engagement in these spaces are evident in the young men's critique of the lack of accountability within online gaming environments for addressing hostility and abuse, the emotional toll of online hostility and how exposure to negativity, harassment, and toxic interactions affects their mental health. However, reflexivity towards ethical engagement seems to be limited when it comes to understanding the gendered dimensions of online abuse and how such abuse impacts others. Toxic gaming cultures, for instance, are normalised as part of competitive male spaces, with some of the young men viewing trash talk and aggression as an expected and accepted component of the gaming experience.

Concerns with ethical engagement are also evident in the young men's efforts to disengage from toxic digital spaces. Many consciously decide to step away from negativity, avoid online arguments, or refrain from contributing to harmful discourse. Some reflect on their past participation in toxic cultures, acknowledging how their digital behaviours have evolved over time. These reflections indicate an ethical awareness around individual responsibility in shaping online environments. However, ethical engagement seems to be weak when it comes to collective responsibility. While the young men recognise the harms of online toxicity, few discuss taking active steps to challenge these cultures. Many view disengagement as the primary solution, rather than exploring alternative forms of intervention, resistance, or community-building.

Conclusion

This chapter has highlighted the contradictory nature of young men's experiences of connection, community, and conflict online. Digital spaces offer belonging, support, and acceptance—from family and friendship groups to gaming communities and queer networks. However, they are also sites of hostility, toxicity, and exclusion. The analysis drew attention to the curatorial intentionality, scepticism, ethical engagement, and reflexivity within the young men's engagements as they curated platforms and communities to sustain positive ties and protect their wellbeing. Yet their accounts also exposed the normalisation of abuse and the limits of individual strategies in the face of platform architectures that amplify negativity. While many sought to disengage from harmful spaces, few challenged the broader cultures that sustain online hostility. The following chapter examines young men's concerns about being led astray or misinformed online.

References

Adinolf, S., & Türkay, S. (2018). Toxic behaviors in esports games: Player perceptions and coping strategies. In *Proceedings of the 2018 annual symposium on computer-human interaction in play companion extended abstracts (CHI PLAY '18 extended abstracts)* (pp. 365–372). Association for Computing Machinery.

Archard, S. J. (2014). Feeling connected: A sense of belonging and social presence in an online community of learners. *International Journal of Cyber Ethics in Education (IJCEE), 3*(2), 16–28.

Beres, N., Frommel, J., Reid, E. Mandryk, R., & Klarkowski, M. (2021). Don't you know that you're toxic: Normalization of toxicity in online gaming. In

Proceedings of the 2021 CHI conference on human factors in computing systems (CHI '21) (Article 438 1–15). Association for Computing Machinery.

Braithwaite, A. (2016). It's about ethics in games journalism? Gamergaters and geek masculinity. *Social Media + Society, 2*, 1–10.

Brodie, J., & Osowska, R. (2021). Supporting entrepreneurship students' sense of belonging in online virtual spaces. *Industry and Higher Education, 35*(4), 353–359.

Byron, P., Robards, B., Hanckel, B., Vivienne, S., & Churchill, B. (2019). Hey, I'm having these experiences: Tumblr use and young people's queer (dis)connections. *International Journal of Communication, 13*, 2239–2259.

Castaño-Pulgarín, S. A., Suárez-Betancur, N., Vega, L. M. T., & López, H. M. H. (2021). Internet, social media and online hate speech. Systematic review. *Aggression and Violent Behavior, 58*, 101608.

Davis, K. (2012). Tensions of identity in a networked era: Young people's perspectives on the risks and rewards of online self-expression. *New Media & Society, 14*(4), 634–651.

Dørum, K., Bartle, C., & Pennington, M. (2010). The effect of online social networking on facilitating sense of belonging among university students living off campus. In J. Herrington & C. Montgomerie (Eds.), *Proceedings of ED-MEDIA 2010—World conference on educational multimedia, hypermedia & telecommunications* (pp. 529–535). Association for the Advancement of Computing in Education (AACE).

Fu, J. (2018). Chinese youth performing identities and navigating belonging online. *Journal of Youth Studies, 21*(2), 129–143.

Fuss, B.G., Dorstyn, D. and Ward, L. (2021). 'Belonging in the Online World: Older Adults' Use of Internet for Community.', *Journal of Social Inclusion, 12*(2), p. 3–29.

Geena Davis Institute, Oak Foundation, & Equimundo. (2021). *The double edged sword of online gaming: An analysis of masculinity in video games and the gaming community*. Geena Davis Institute, Oak Foundation & Equimundo.

Hanckel, B., & Morris, A. (2014). Finding community and contesting heteronormativity: Queer young people's engagement in an Australian online community. *Journal of Youth Studies, 17*(7), 872–886.

Kaye, L. S., Hellsten, L. M., McIntyre, L., & Hendry, B. (2022). 'There's a fine line between trash-talking and cyberbullying': A qualitative exploration of youth perspectives of online gaming culture. *International Review of Sociology, 32*, 426–442.

Keddie, A., & Bartel, D. (2021). The affective intensities of gender transformative work: An actionable framework for facilitators working with boys and young men. *Journal of Men and Masculinities, 24*(5), 740–759.

Lemercier-Dugarin, M., Romo, L., Tijus, C., & Zerhouni, O. (2021). "Who are the Cyka Blyat?" How empathy, impulsivity, and motivations to play predict aggressive behaviors in multiplayer online games. *Cyberpsychology, Behavior, and Social Networking, 24*(1), 63–69.

Light, B. (2013). Networked masculinities and social networking sites: A call for the analysis of men and contemporary digital. *Masculinities and Social Change, 2*(3), 245–265.

Maharani, A., Puspita, V., Aurora, R. A., & Wiranito, N. (2024). Understanding toxicity in online gaming: A focus on communication based behaviours towards female players in Valorant. *Jurnal Syntax Admiration, 5*(5), 1559–1567.

Massanari, A. (2017). #Gamergate and the fappening: How Reddit's algorithm, governance, and culture support toxic technocultures. *New Media & Society, 19*(3), 329–346.

Pangrazio, L. (2018). *Young people's literacies in the digital age: Continuities, conflicts and contradictions.* Routledge.

Peacock, S., Cowan, J., Irvine, L., & Williams, J. (2020). An exploration into the importance of a sense of belonging for online learners. *The International Review of Research in Open and Distance Learning, 21*(2), 18–35.

Pietersen, A. J., Coetzee, J., Byczkowska-Owczarek, D., & Elliker, F. (2019). Online gamers, lived experiences, and sense of belonging: Students at the University of the Free State, Bloemfontein. *Qualitative Sociology Review, 14*(4), 122–137.

Siegel, A. A. (2020). Online hate speech. In N. Perslity & J. A. Tucker (Eds.), *Social media and democracy: The state of the field, prospects for reform* (pp. 56–88). Cambridge University Press.

Siegel, A. A., Nikitin, E., Barberá, P., Sterling, J., Pullen, B., Bonneau, R., Nagler, J., & Tucker, J. A. (2019). *Trumping hate on Twitter? Online hate in the 2016 US election and its aftermath.* Social Media and Political Participation, New York University.

Twenge, J. M. (2013). Does online social media lead to social connection or social disconnection? *Journal of College and Character, 14*(1), 11–20.

Weinstein, E., & James, C. (2022). *Behind their screens: What teens are facing and adults are missing.* The MIT Press.

Zsila, A., Shabahang, R., Aruguete, M. S., & Orosz, G. (2022). Toxic behaviors in online multiplayer games: Prevalence, perception, risk factors of victimization, and psychological consequences. *Aggressive Behavior, 48*(3), 356–364.

CHAPTER 4

Being Led Astray or Misinformed

Abstract This chapter explores the young men's concerns about being led astray or misinformed online. These concerns are associated with the negative influence of algorithms shaping their online experiences. While some appreciated consuming content curated by algorithms, others expressed scepticism that algorithms may steer them towards unwelcome or harmful content. The young men's critical awareness of algorithms prompted some to proactively curate content to avoid becoming stuck in echo chambers. In relation to misinformation, the chapter foregrounds the young men's views about credible and false information online, their embracing but also scepticism of the gendered content peddled by the controversial influencer Andrew Tate, and their thoughts about freedom of expression, cancel culture and censorship. The analytic summaries interspersed within the chapter draw attention to practices of curatorial intentionality, scepticism, ethical engagement and reflexivity [Pangrazio, L. (2018). *Young people's literacies in the digital age: Continuities, conflicts and contradictions*. Routledge].

Keywords Young men • Misinformation • Algorithms • Online engagements • Gendered content • Freedom of expression • Cancel culture • Censorship

A. Keddie, M. Flood, *Young Men's Online Lives*,
https://doi.org/10.1007/978-3-031-99980-2_4

Concerns About the Negative Influence of Algorithms

The young men expressed concern about the negative impacts of algorithms. They viewed algorithms as online architectures that encouraged particular views and beliefs—as curating what they see online. While a few of the young men expressed positive views about algorithms, for example, Nate (18, S, CALD) expressed appreciation for how the content he gets on his feed aligns with his interests, most of the young men who mentioned algorithms were critical of the way they worked. Campbell (18, B, D) raised concern about the influence of algorithms in leading people down rabbit holes where they can encounter potentially harmful content, as he explained:

> I feel like there are some people that might be influenced by it [algorithms] more so than me because I know I watch these videos [and] I just like acknowledge how stupid some of this stuff… is but then I guess the way the TikTok algorithm works is that they would associate the watch time with necessarily being engaged by it [and] then they give you more and more. (Campbell, 18, B, D)

Similarly, Felix (20, B) expressed concern about algorithms that curate content based on user preferences, noting that this can lead to the reinforcement of negative ideologies and behaviours. He stated:

> It's pretty concerning to me … the way social media and online platforms are designed is to increase engagement and the fact that they can so effectively target the demographics that will engage with that content and just continue to feed it to them … I think it perpetuates some pretty negative ideologies, definitely like, sexism is a pretty key one [for example] … if Andrew Tate is your role model, it's pretty concerning and I think it would be pretty easy to pick that up as a role model, whether you want to or not, if you watch that kind of content, and you accept that as the norm, you know, that's not something that you're necessarily in control of … you don't start watching Andrew Tate and be like, "Oh, I want to think this way". It's just something that happens the more content you consume. (Felix, 20, B)

Tim (17, S, CALD) also raised concerns about algorithms and their impact on his online feed. He described how he sometimes finds himself going down rabbit holes where his entire feed changes, possibly due to the algorithm's recommendations. To regain control over his feed, he spoke of actively using the "not interested" function on specific platforms. Christian (17, S, D) pointed out that algorithms can have a negative effect on younger people in relation to limiting their perspectives. He noted that algorithms often prioritise content that aligns with users' existing views, thus "kind of affirming your voice instead of things that challenge and that can kind of lead to [broader] perspectives". Charlie (19, S) similarly highlighted the intentions of algorithms, especially those on Instagram to "keep you online". He noted how personalised algorithms encourage users to keep scrolling and engaging with content and that this reinforces existing beliefs "because you're only being fed content from that perspective".

Other young men in the study were also critical of the working and impact of algorithms. Benito (20, S, CALD) became concerned about algorithms after watching a documentary about how effectively they entice users and keep them engaged. He reported, "it opened my eyes a bit", how the algorithm, "draws you in", and how well "it actually reads" your interests. He started monitoring his screen time as a response to limit his "excessive" use. Ian (21, G) mentioned how algorithms, particularly in advertising, can be invasive and "pretty scary" because they can track users' interests and then bombard them with tailored ads. While Ian noted that this can be helpful in some cases, he also expressed the view that it feels like "an invasion of your privacy at times".

Nathan (17, S) highlighted the addictive nature of algorithms, particularly on platforms like TikTok, where the "For You" page continuously feeds content tailored to user preferences. This endless stream of content, he commented, is "almost addictive, in a sense, because it just doesn't end". Phil (16, S) noted how he actively fed algorithms by subscribing to various channels and consuming content on platforms like YouTube, while Scott (16, S) shared his annoyance with algorithms that sometimes present content contrary to his views. He spoke about how he navigates these algorithms, stating, "I just get a lot of random stuff. It's like in between like gaming and … then like, right-wing stuff because of course when you look at the comments, on like something the algorithm thinks you like [it]" and will send you more, "it's kind of annoying."

These comments point to the young men's critical awareness of how algorithms shape their online experiences. First, they recognise how algorithms can amplify harmful and extreme content, including materials that may negatively impact their behaviour. Second, they recognise how algorithms create filter bubbles and echo chambers that limit exposure to diverse perspectives, potentially amplifying extreme political ideologies and polarisation. Third, they recognise how social media algorithms are designed to keep users engaged for long periods, leading to mindless scrolling, time wasting, and potential addiction, a concern among young men that we explored in Chap. 2.

Young men's awareness of how algorithms may encourage and intensify sexism, however, is less visible, with only one participant (Felix) commenting on this at any length. Online platforms' algorithms can propagate and amplify sexist ideologies. For example, algorithms may encourage the presentation of stereotypically gendered content and reinforce traditional gender roles and identities (Gerrard & Thornham, 2020). Advertising algorithms may perpetuate gender biases, with one study finding a preference for headless women in ads (Cecere et al., 2018), or result in gender-biased ad delivery, for example of job advertisements, even when the intent is gender-neutral (Lambrecht & Tucker, 2019), or reflect the gender biases in the text collections on which they are based and thus associate negative attributes more often with women than men (Rathee et al., 2023). Algorithmic biases even extend to music streaming services such as Spotify, where recommendation algorithms create gendered listening experiences (Werner, 2020).

Social media platforms such as YouTube, TikTok, and Instagram use algorithms that recommend misogynistic and anti-feminist content to male users, as four recent studies have documented.

- A 2021 study found that YouTube's recommendation system steers users towards videos related to Incels, an online sub-culture based on misogyny and anti-feminism (Papadamou et al., 2021). Users had a 6.3% chance of being suggested an Incel-related video by YouTube's recommendation algorithm within five hops when starting from a non Incel-related video.
- A 2022 Australian study set up ten mock male YouTube accounts and found that all were recommended videos with sexist and anti-feminist content. Following the recommendations and viewing and liking this suggested content resulted in recommendations for more bluntly misogynist content. This phenomenon was worse on YouTube shorts (which feature shorter videos), with this platform

showing more extreme videos in shorter time frames (Thomas & Balint, 2022).

- A 2024 UK study created a series of mock accounts on TikTok for teenage boys, with distinct content interests typical of common profiles, e.g., seeking out content on masculinity or addressing loneliness. The content in the videos that TikTok suggested in its "For You" page initially was in line with these content interests, but then increasingly focused on anger and blame directed at women. After five days, the TikTok algorithm was presenting four times as many videos with misogynistic content such as objectification, sexual harassment or discrediting women (Regehr et al., 2024).
- In a 2024 Irish study involving ten fake profiles of young men for TikTok and YouTube shorts, misogynist manosphere content was sent to users regardless of whether those accounts actively searched for it (Baker et al., 2024). This was especially the case for the profiles set up to model teenage boys seeking out content typically associated with masculine gender norms. All accounts were presented with patriarchal and anti-feminist content, and the frequency increased once their account demonstrated interest or engagement.

The young men in this study did show some awareness of algorithms' promotion of harmful or extreme content. In response, some had adopted vigilant content curation to counter algorithmic echo chambers, a strategy also visible among other young people (Weinstein & James, 2022). The reflections on addiction, privacy invasion, and the inadvertent shaping of perspectives showcase a nuanced understanding of the complex interplay between user agency and algorithmic influence (Pangrazio, 2018).

Regarding the elements of critical digital literacy, the comments in this section demonstrate curatorial intentionality in the young men's active selection and filtering of their online content to shape and manage their digital experiences. Such intentionality is informed by scepticism, particularly towards the manipulative design and ideological reinforcement of algorithms. It is also informed by concerns about ethical engagement. The young men were critical of how social media algorithms target specific demographics and reinforce harmful ideologies, such as misogynistic content linked to figures like Andrew Tate as well as recognising the ways in which algorithms limit exposure to diverse viewpoints, reinforcing existing biases rather than promoting critical thought. Scepticism and a desire for ethical engagement were further apparent in the young men's criticism of the privacy-invading nature of targeted advertising and in their self-critical stance on their own digital consumption, evident for example, in their recognition that they could be influenced by algorithmic content even when they initially dismissed it as "stupid".

Concerns About Misinformation and Misrepresentation

Many of the young men in this research expressed concerns about the issue of misinformation online. Several emphasised the importance of critical thinking and the need to be cautious when consuming information on the internet. Jordan (16, S), for example, acknowledged the overwhelming presence of both information and misinformation on various online platforms. He highlighted the challenge of distinguishing between what is true and what is not: "it can be difficult at times to sift through it all and, you know, take in and digest what you believe to be true and what you don't". Jordan noted the potential for this misinformation to negatively affect people's mental state, as he explained:

> [There's a] lot of just crap, basically just this stuff that is just there to be there. I don't know, it can kind of mess with your brain a little bit ... it's all about how you handle it, I guess, and ... if you're capable of recognising when it's, you know, just nonsense, and when it is like legitimate news and stuff. (Jordan, 16, S)

Warren (18, S) expressed scepticism about online information, suggesting that the pursuit of profit often trumps accuracy in the media landscape. He implied that news outlets may sometimes embellish details or spread falsehoods to gain attention and retain viewership: "they're all trying to make money, and the way to make money is to gain attention and retain attention and if making up a few details gets the attention, then yeah, who cares?"

Ibrahim (18, S, CALD) similarly pointed out that misinformation can be most dangerous when it reaches people who lack the critical thinking skills to discern fact from fiction. He highlighted young people as a particularly vulnerable group in this context, as they may absorb and internalise false information, making it challenging to change their beliefs, especially if exposed to misinformation from an early age. Gavin (20, S) also reflected on the importance of individuals who can recognise and combat misinformation online.

Young people are more likely to encounter misinformation than older people as they increasingly rely on social media as their main news source, as Australian data documents (Notley et al., 2023). Young men's concerns about misinformation are shared with others in Australia, with a recent survey finding that 75% of adults in Australia feel concerned about misinformation (Park et al., 2021). There has been a rise in the degree of concern, both in Australia (from 64% in 2022), and globally, from 52% to 58% over 2022 to 2024 across a range of countries (Park et al., 2021). Population rates of concern about misinformation vary globally, and concern is highest in countries with liberal democratic governments (Knuutila et al., 2022).

Other studies with younger cohorts have found low levels of confidence or skill in the ability to recognise and avoid misinformation. For example, an Australian survey found that less than half (41%) of young people aged 8–16 agreed that they know how to tell fake news stories from real stories, 28% said they cannot do this, and 31% were unsure. Young people were more likely to say they can tell real from fake news stories if they were older (13–16), had parents with higher levels of education, or had more interest in news (Notley et al., 2023). Another Australian study found that high school students often struggle to recognise bias, particularly when it relates to political or organisational affiliations. They frequently fail to verify accuracy or authority outside of social media posts and tend to trust "evidence" even when it is inaccurate (Johnston, 2020).

The young men in our study seem more confident of their ability to recognise and avoid misinformation than the young people in these other studies, but this may reflect their older age, the study sample, or other factors. One factor may be over-confidence. Various studies describe young people as excessively confident of their own abilities to identify and avoid misinformation, and as showing a 'third person effect' in which they think it is others, not themselves, who are more likely to be deceived (Zozaya-Durazo et al., 2024). A recent UK study among young people in high schools found that a higher proportion of boys than girls claim to be able to spot misinformation and fake news online, but speculated that this may indicate higher confidence rather than ability (Katz & Asam, 2023).

The young men also expressed concern and engaged in critique about what they viewed as misrepresentation (as opposed to misinformation) online. Again, Andrew Tate was a topic of discussion that generated contention amongst the participants. Several of the young men spoke in defence of Tate, critical of what they viewed as an unfairly negative misrepresentation of his views. Manny (18, S) for example, commented that media agencies actively misrepresent Tate's views as "extremely negative", painting Tate in a "bad light" as "misogynistic" and taking his views "out of context". Jordan (16, S) too stated that the media focuses on the negative aspects of Tate's content, ignoring his positive content on personal development, as he explained: "I don't really think I've ever heard anything positive in like the mainstream media about him". One factor that may shape young men's perceptions of Tate as misrepresented is that much of his written content focuses on men and masculinities and a project of self-improvement, rather than explicit attacks on women and feminism, although its content still serves to support and defend men's domination over women (Roberts et al., 2025).

Another common line of commentary among the young men, less endorsing of Tate's views but still softening a critique of them, also focused on the claim that he is misrepresented, but attributed this to the general dynamics of the online world where people's circulation of particularly controversial segments of media content fuels misrepresentation or influencers themselves court controversy to generate views and engagement. As Isaiah (21, S, CALD) commented:

> [Tate] is very controversial again, but then what happens is they'll take that one clip from him, that particular controversial line, and then they'll extrapolate from him that particular controversial line, and then they'll extrapolate it to something very big. And then, the polarisation happens from there like guys and girls are divided. (Isaiah, 21, S, CALD)

Some young men understood Tate as exploiting his notoriety and status as a misogynist and polarising figure for financial gain, that is, as a ploy to generate clicks, views, and revenue. Tariq (19, S) commented:

> I mean it is kind of in [Tate's] best interest to be controversial because the way the world we're kind of living in, the greatest kind of asset you can have is attention right? So, by [being] all controversial and saying things that usually people don't say, you will stir up the pot, you will get lots of views, likes, comments. ... Tate's not just doing this for fun. I mean, he has something to sell his audience. So of course, he's gonna be controversial, get people on. And eventually get more sales. (Tariq, 19, S)

Similarly, Cedric (18, S) stated that, "yeah, I find he says things to grab people's attention. And like he'll say something outrageous. It'll get the news on him. It'll get all the attention." Similarly, Henry (16, S) proposed that Tate states controversial views to "get reactions" and thus to make money, stating, "he also knows that when people are getting mad and criticising him, he's making money for that".

Social media influencers use a variety of strategies to engage followers: providing value, creating emotional bonds, interacting and co-creating with followers, and disclosing their personal lives (Lou & Zhou, 2024). However, a strategy used by some includes posting deliberately controversial content in the hope that it will attract attention, thus leveraging 'outrage culture' for attention and followers (Lok, 2019). As these young men speculate, Tate's more controversial posts may reflect this strategy.

For several of the young men, the misrepresentation and public damnation of Tate reflected a general censoring and silencing of men within online and offline spaces. Tariq (19, S) referred to Tate as boldly saying what others have been unable to say in a climate of media censorship: "No one else has been saying this. Everyone else has been silenced … [Tate is] this bold guy just changing the course of the entire internet right". This account may reflect a narrative that Tate himself offers, that he is standing up for his beliefs in an authentic way and is a voice of reason on gender equality. This narrative aligns with traditional norms of masculinity, and other research among 13–14-year old boys in the UK also documents its popularity (Haslop et al., 2024). The notion that men now are being censored and silenced, and indeed that 'it is getting difficult to be a straight white man', has increasing currency in some online forums (Hanson et al., 2023), and some of the young men in our study echo this.

Some young men who viewed Tate positively also reported self-censoring views similar to his in their interactions with others because of their awareness that these views would be unwelcome. As Warren (18, S) reported, "in normal life especially, it's it's kind of where I have to shut my mouth, because I'm quite supportive of lots of things [he says]".

A wider theme that emerged here is freedom of expression on the internet, with some of the young men commenting on cancel culture (the practice of withdrawing support from a person, group, or organisation due to their actions or opinions being considered offensive, often on social media platforms) and political correctness. Some young men condemned cancel culture, while others expressed ambivalence. Franklin (21, S), for example, voiced his dislike for cancel culture, emphasising that it restricts "free speech." Maxie (21, S, CALD) also expressed reservations about cancel culture, feeling that people on the internet are overly sensitive. He commented that there should be room for individuals to express their opinions and that cancel culture has shifted from calling out genuinely outrageous statements to stifling free expression, as he explained:

> Yeah, not the biggest fan of [cancel culture]. I feel like everyone these days are a little bit too sensitive on the internet. I can't tell if it's just me being insensitive or the other way around but yeah, just I feel like anyone should be allowed to say stuff within reason and I thought cancel culture used to be something good that like, if someone said something genuinely outrageous, it will be called out … now it's just like people can't say stuff. Basically, you can never say something without at least having someone on the internet disagree and try to ruin your life. (Maxie, 21, S, CALD)

Brodie (20, B) was similarly conflicted:

> like we should both be able to like, you know, argue with each other … but like I do think that sometimes it goes a bit far, like when people accuse someone of like being malicious when they actually just didn't know, they didn't understand like, you know, it's, you know, everyone's job to kind of maybe like educate them and like help them understand. (Brodie, 20, B)

The concerns raised by the young men in this section regarding online misinformation and misrepresentation highlight the crucial role of critical thinking in navigating the digital landscape (Pangrazio, 2018; Weinstein & James, 2022). The young men highlighted the prevalence of misinformation, emphasising the need to distinguish between credible and false information. Their critical reflections extend beyond misinformation to include a nuanced examination of the representation of controversial figures, such as influencer Andrew Tate. The young men recognised the potential for misrepresentation, contending that Tate's views are distorted, especially in mainstream media. However, this defence of Tate raises questions about the perpetuation of harmful masculine norms. Here many young men's critical focus is on defending Tate rather than recognising and challenging the harm in his sexist and misogynistic messages, just as other scholarship among young men finds both critical responses to and affirmations of patriarchal gender norms (Doull et al., 2013; Flood, 2018; Ravn & Roberts, 2019). The participants' observations regarding Tate's deliberate use of controversy for financial gain exemplify their critical views about the monetisation of polarising narratives online. The young men's feelings of being censored in their offline and online worlds are concerning as open communication and dialogue are central to any form of social change. The tensions between cancel culture and free expression add further complexity to the dialogue, with perspectives of opposition and ambivalence (Weinstein & James, 2022).

The young men's engagement with critical digital dispositions in this section, like earlier sections, reflects an active curation of their digital experiences, selectively consuming content that aligns with their beliefs while critiquing mainstream media for biased portrayals. For some of the young men, such practice is driven by a reflexive process of scepticism and a desire for ethical engagement—e.g., the young men are critical of and question misinformation online and they express awareness of how misinformation is generated through the pursuit of profit. In relation to Andrew Tate, for example, such scepticism plays out in ambivalent ways—while some of the young men defend the media's 'unfair' and incomplete representation of him, some recognise Tate's deliberate attempts to exploit his notoriety as a misogynist while others champion his message as standing up for men. As with the earlier sections, this scepticism seems to be informed by the young men's desire for ethical engagement (what they see as important and good for them). However, this desire for ethics, while extending to a concern for others (who are unable to detect and resist misinformation) does not extend to considering the gendered dimensions of misinformation (especially in relation to Tate) in terms of its impacts on girls and women.

Conclusion

This chapter has highlighted young men's concerns about being led astray or misinformed online. Although, algorithms were valued for tailoring content to interests, they were more often criticised as encouraging addictive behaviours and reinforcing narrow and sometimes harmful views through the creation of echo chambers. Curatorial intentionality, scepticism, ethical engagement, and reflexivity were evident in the young men's efforts to resist algorithmic influence and to question the credibility of online information. However, their reflections also exposed a sense of ambivalence, particularly in relation to Andrew Tate, where some defended his 'misrepresentation', sidelining or ignoring the harms of his misogynistic content. While many of the young men expressed concerns about misinformation and cancel culture, managing these concerns tended to be framed in terms of personal freedom and individual responsibility, with little attention to the broader gendered impacts of digital misrepresentation. The following chapter explores the young men's experiences of sex, intimacy and privacy in online spaces.

References

Baker, C., Ging, D., & Brandt Andreasen, M. (2024). *Recommending toxicity: The role of algorithmic recommender functions on YouTube Shorts and TikTok in promoting male supremacist influencers.* https://antibullyingcentre.ie/wp-content/uploads/2024/04/DCU-Recommending-Toxicity-Summary-Report.pdf

Cecere, G., Jean, C., Manant, M., & Tucker, C. (2018). Computer algorithms prefer headless women. *2018 MIT CODE: Conference on digital experimentation*, Oct 2018, Boston.

Doull, M., Oliffe, J., Knight, R., & Shoveller, J. A. (2013). Sex and straight young men: Challenging and endorsing hegemonic masculinities and gender regimes. *Men and Masculinities, 16*(3), 329–346.

Flood, M. (2018). Men and the man box—A commentary. In The Men's Project & M. Flood (Eds.), *The man box: A study on being a young man in Australia* (pp. 46–53). Jesuit Social Services.

Gerrard, Y., & Thornham, H. (2020). Content moderation: Social media's sexist assemblages. *New Media & Society, 22*(7), 1266–1286. https://doi.org/10.1177/1461444820912540

Hanson, K. R., Pascoe, C. J., & Light, R. (2023). "It's getting difficult to be a straight White man": Bundled masculinity grievances on reddit. *Sex Roles, 88*(3), 169–186.

Haslop, C., Ringrose, J., Cambazoglu, I., & Milne, B. (2024). Mainstreaming the manosphere's misogyny through affective homosocial currencies. *Social Media & Society, 10*(1). https://doi.org/10.1177/20563051241228811

Johnston, N. (2020). Living in the world of fake news: High school students' evaluation of information from social media sites. *Journal of the Australian Library and Information Association, 69*(4), 430–450.

Katz, A., & Asam, A. E. (2023). *Real or fake? Teenagers managing life on screens.* Youthworks.

Knuutila, A., Neudert, L. M., & Howard, P. N. (2022). Who is afraid of fake news?: Modeling risk perceptions of misinformation in 142 countries. *Harvard Kennedy School Misinformation Review, 3*(3), 1–13.

Park, S., Fisher, C., McGuinness, K., Lee, J., McCallum, K., Cai, X., Chatskin, M., Mardjianto, L., & Yao, P. (2024). Digital news report: Australia 2024. News and Media Research Centre University of Canberra.

Lambrecht, A., & Tucker, C. (2019). Algorithmic bias? An empirical study of apparent gender-based discrimination in the display of STEM career ads. *Management Science, 65*(7), 2966–2981.

Lok, D. (2019, December 22). *How influencers are using negative attention to create the bandwagon effect, and why it works.* https://danlok.com/influencers-are-using-negative-attention-to-create-bandwagon-effect/

Lou, C., & Zhou, X. (2024). What else is new about social media influencers? Uncovering their relation and content strategies, and the downsides of being famous. *Frontiers in Psychology, 15,* 1437384. https://doi.org/10.3389/fpsyg.2024.1437384

Notley, T., Chambers, S., Zhong, H. F., Park, S., Lee, J. Y., & Dezuanni, M. (2023). *News and young Australians in 2023: How children and teens access, perceive and are affected by news media.* Western Sydney University.

Pangrazio, L. (2018). *Young people's literacies in the digital age: Continuities, conflicts and contradictions.* Routledge.

Papadamou, K., Zannettou, S., Blackburn, J., De Cristofaro, E., Stringhini, G., & Sirivianos, M. (2021). Understanding the Incel community on YouTube. *Proceeding of the ACM on human-computer interaction.*

Rathee, S., Banker, S., Mishra, A., and Mishra, H. (2023). Algorithms propagate gender bias in the marketplace—with consumers' co operation. *Journal of Consumer Psychology 33*(4): 621–631.

Ravn, S., & Roberts, S. (2019). Young masculinities: Masculinities in youth studies. In L. Gottzén, U. Mellström, & T. Shefer (Eds.), *Routledge international handbook of masculinity studies* (pp. 183–191). Routledge.

Regehr, K., Shaughnessy, C., Zhao, M., & Shaughnessy, N. (2024). *Safer scrolling: How algorithms popularise and gamify online hate and misogyny for young people.* University College London (UCL) and the University of Kent.

Roberts, S., Jones, C., Nicholas, L., Wescott, S., & Maloney, M. (2025). Beyond the clickbait: Analysing the masculinist ideology in Andrew Tate's online written discourses. *Cultural Sociology.* https://doi.org/10.1177/17499755241307414

Thomas, E., & Balint, K. (2022). *Algorithms as a weapon against women: How YouTube lures boys and young men into the 'manosphere'.* Reset Tech Australia and the Institute for Strategic Dialogue.

Weinstein, E., & James, C. (2022). *Behind their screens: What teens are facing and adults are missing.* The MIT Press.

Werner, A. (2020). Organizing music, organizing gender: Algorithmic culture and Spotify recommendations. *Popular Communication, 18*(1), 78–90.

Zozaya-Durazo, L. D., Sádaba-Chalezquer, C., & Feijoo-Fernández, B. (2024). "Fake or not, I'm sharing it": Teen perception about disinformation in social networks. *Young Consumers, 25*(4), 425–438.

CHAPTER 5

Sex, Intimacy and Privacy

Abstract This chapter examines sex, intimacy and privacy. It foregrounds the young men's concerns about the accessibility and consumption of online pornography in relation to its ubiquity and infiltration in their everyday online experiences. They present an overwhelmingly negative picture of how online pornography impacts on their lives including struggles with addiction, desensitisation towards explicit content, distorted views of sex and sexual consent, the objectification of women's bodies and the degradation of their relationships with girls and women. The chapter also foregrounds the young men's concerns about privacy and safety online, noting issues ranging from online scams targeting family members to personal encounters with catfishing. The discussions around the regulation and censorship of online content highlight the struggle these young men experience in striking a balance between user protection and freedom of expression. The chapter includes analytic summaries to draw attention to curatorial intentionality, scepticism, ethical engagement and reflexivity [Pangrazio, L. (2018). *Young people's literacies in the digital age: Continuities, conflicts and contradictions*. Routledge].

Keywords Young men • Sex • Intimacy • Online pornography • Privacy • Safety

A. Keddie, M. Flood, *Young Men's Online Lives*,
https://doi.org/10.1007/978-3-031-99980-2_5

Concerns with the Accessibility of Pornography

Exposure to and use of pornography is routine among young men. Males are more likely than females to intentionally use pornography, to do so regularly, and to first view it at a young age (Crabbe et al., 2024; eSafety Commissioner, 2023). In an Australian study of 15–29-year-olds, 100% of males and 82% of females reported ever viewing pornography (Lim et al., 2017). In another study among young people aged 15–20, over four-fifths (86%) of young men and over two-thirds (69%) of young women had seen pornography. That same study found that many young men are frequent users, with over half (54.4%) using pornography at least weekly and one in six (16%) doing so daily, whereas young women's use is far less frequent (with 14.3% using pornography weekly and only 1.4% doing so daily) (Crabbe et al., 2024). More widely, the use of pornography has become increasingly normalised among young people, particularly young men. Among young people, males are more likely than females to see pornography use as 'normal' and acceptable, while females are more likely to be concerned about and more negative towards pornography, as documented in research in the UK (Martellozzo et al., 2016), US (Carroll et al., 2008), New Zealand (Meehan, 2023), and Sweden (Löfgren-Mårtenson & Månsson, 2010). Young men use pornography for a variety of reasons, including, for example, as a source of sexual gratification and sexual pleasure, as sexual education, as a form of leisure, to relieve boredom, and to bond with friends (McCormack & Wignall, 2017).

Although the young men in our research were not forthcoming about their own use of pornography, many did raise concerns about the ubiquity of online pornography and its effects (eSafety Commissioner, 2023). Quinn (20, S) noted the prevalence of explicit content on the internet and the challenge of avoiding it: "I think it just comes down to the, you know, [what] the internet is these days. You've got everything everywhere". Ibrahim (18, S, CALD) also commented on issues of accessibility and how algorithms worked to "push young men" towards viewing explicit content. He noted that pornography "bleeds into" every facet of online spaces, and that despite pressing "not interested" to pornographic content on Instagram it is still recommended to him.

Lucas (18, S) described how sexually explicit content infiltrates everyday online activities like scrolling through TikTok or Instagram. It often appears unexpectedly, potentially pushing individuals toward consuming more adult content. Similarly, Jamie (16, First Nations) referred to the ubiquity of explicit content in his everyday online life:

> ... so like just to really put into perspective how much it's really gone into our culture ... the other day I was scrolling through and like there was an Uber Ad and it was like, you can get a vibrator on Uber Eats. I'm like, come on man, if I'm on Uber Eats, all I want is like a Pepsi or some shit, like I don't need the vibrator! (Jamie, 16, First Nations)

To the extent that the young men identified harmful impacts of pornography exposure or use, these involved addiction and brain development, negative views of women, distorted views of consent, and premature exposure to sexualised content. Several of the young men spoke of how their access to online pornography at an early age had affected them negatively, including offering narratives of addiction. Jamie (16, First Nations), who first encountered pornography at 11 years old, noted how this exposure and the saturation of adult content online more broadly is desensitising and can lead to struggles with "addiction":

> a lot of people nowadays ... have struggles with porn addiction and I feel like that itself has a big impact on the way we perceive content. And yeah, there's a lot of unsolicited stuff that you see scrolling through which is mostly just advertising and all the main pages that post photos of like these chicks ... I guess definitely desensitising ... it's so accessible and it's such a common subject when it really isn't that important. Life shouldn't be that. (Jamie, 16, First Nations)

Toby (16, S) opened up about being exposed to online pornography "from the age of around 10". He explained:

> unfortunately, I was one of those victims, because I did see it on social media, you know, I got curious and then it's taken me six years and just now I've been just able to get over it, but the point is that's how much of a toll it takes, it's, you know, it really can be a bit of [an] addiction. (Toby, 16, S)

Kieran (19, S) also described his relationship with pornography as an addiction. He shared his personal battle with this addiction, emphasising the negative impact it had on his perception of girls and his ability to maintain healthy relationships:

> I was first exposed around 13 … I didn't really know how to manage any of that, and hormones is a new thing, so I kinda got addicted and so that was a pretty negative thing for me that went on for a few years up and down … and so I've kind of always seen it as negative, even though I was addicted the whole time … like most addictions, you want to stop, and you feel ashamed every time but you can't … not feeling capable of being able to stop is a very, very shameful and a real crap mental spot to be in … and that would negatively impact the way I saw, yeah girls around me, you know, like I'm, I would never make an advance on anyone or never actually mistreat them but just small things like picturing girls who, like good friends, but very platonic friends, just actually naked and that … and that happened because of that addiction. Yeah, and you know, and then it didn't really stop until I did get in a relationship, and where I finally was able to talk to my girlfriend about the fact that, 'Hey, I've been struggling with this for a few years' and so, you know, like it negatively impacted that relationship for a little bit there. (Kieran, 19, S)

Brendan (20, S) similarly commented on the negative impacts of pornography when he was young. He explained:

> … when you [are] that young, you don't even realise any of this shit, like what it's doing to you … like, now [I'm] older, I look [back], okay, this is bad, like this, a lot of studies and shit showing, this is like bad for your brain, like you're fucking yourself up a bit here. But I think when you're young, you don't know the impacts. So that's sort of a desensitising. Getting kind of I guess addicted to it like because some people do it a lot man and when you're a kid like it's hard to self-control and, you know, you're doing it in your room or like you're doing [it] away from everyone so no one else knows. (Brendan, 20, S)

Along these lines, several of the young men noted how pornography dulled their emotional reactions to explicit content, as Scott (16, S) explained: "I was the kid with unrestricted internet access, so I saw a lot of like, a lot of things very early on in my life and I would say that that has really changed me a lot … it's just made me a lot less like reactive to things … I feel like a lot less emotional about things". Jamie (16, First Nations) also spoke of being desensitised: he doesn't "get uncomfortable" seeing adult content, because of his "desensitisation" to such content.

Some of the young men also suggested that pornography is harmful for brain development. Ibrahim (18, S, CALD), commented, for example, "I think it's very toxic like the way it affects your brain is just like any other drug so it's very toxic", while Jordan (16, S) noted, "it's terrible for your brain, your development, especially, you know, at [an early] kind of age ... yeah, that's not what you need when you're still developing and learning concepts about the world". These accounts may reflect the narratives popularised by the "Your Brain on Porn" website and other community-based sites and publications. Jordan (16, S) also commented on the impacts of pornography on the brain as well as on men's mental health:

> ...there really isn't any benefit to [online pornography]. And you know, like, after you've watched it, you just feel terrible, you know, like you feel good watching it but then it's just like immediate regret afterwards. And it's just like ... it's not a good like dopamine cycle for your brain. It just like takes a toll on you over time, and that's why, like a whole lot of young men, you know, have anxiety and depression like around all this stuff as well, because, you know like they, they really don't have a realistic expectation and understanding of what a relationship is. (Jordan, 16, S)

There is no doubt that some users of pornography experience their use as compulsive or damaging in some way. In an Australian study among 15–29-year-olds, around 12% identified their pornography use as problematic, compulsive or concerning, indicating negative impacts on sexual function and relationships (Davis et al., 2017). In another Australian study among people aged 16–69, among respondents who had ever looked at pornography, 4% of men and 1% of women reported that they felt addicted to pornography (Rissel et al., 2017). Some individuals report problematic consumption of pornography, involving impaired control of the extent of their use, neglect of other areas of their life, and persistent use despite damaging psychological effects (de Alarcón et al., 2019). There are debates over whether to understand these as an addiction (Love et al., 2015), an impulse control disorder (de Alarcón et al., 2019), hypersexuality (de Alarcón et al., 2019), or something else. There are also debates and contradictory findings regarding whether pornography is (Jacobs et al., 2021; Park et al., 2016) or is not (Dwulit & Rzymski, 2019; Landripet & Štulhofer, 2015) a significant contributor to men's problems with desire, erection, and orgasm, and if it is, it may be particularly so for men with self-reported problematic use (Grubbs & Gola, 2019). In any case it is clear that, like others, some young men are troubled by their own patterns of pornography use.

Another theme in young men's commentary on pornography was its encouragement of sexist and objectifying views. Several of the young men commented on how pornography had led to negative views about girls and women. Benito (20, S, CALD) noted, especially for younger people, how pornography "twisted with reality" and "changes their perspective on women or certain situations … and I think that's where the damage is". Majak (21, S, CALD) noted how the accessibility and common use of pornography at his high school led to negative ideas about girls and difficulties in making genuine connections, as he explained:

> … when I was in high school, yeah, I went to a boys' school so it was pretty casual the way guys would talk about it … but yeah, guys would just be in the back of the classroom … on the phone … I would say it implants like the wrong idea of how to interact with like girls and stuff. I think it gives you the wrong idea – not that you do anything crazy, but it's sort of, I guess maybe dilutes your mind. I would say to some degree, and it shifts your focus away from just trying to actually make a proper connection and actually trying to get to know somebody. (Majak, 21, S, CALD)

Along similar lines, Nico (18, S, D, CALD) commented that "one of the major effects" from viewing pornography "is that it changes your view of women":

> … it makes you view them more as a sexual object rather than a human being … and I think a lot of people grow up with it, and then they end up not having total respect for women, as just regular people at the end of the day. And it's definitely toxic. It's a bad habit to get into. It's using your energies for something that's not productive. (Nico, 18, S, D, CALD)

In Jordan's (16, S) view, pornography "just really alters expectations of, you know, like what women should be … and, you know, obviously, it's all scripted, and it's fake". Omer (17, S, CALD) shared a similar view, that online pornography "alters a lot of your perspectives on women as well. The second you see one, your first thought is, what would she look like with her clothes off instead of, you know? That's actually a person. I think it's the whole reason behind the objectification in today's society".

Young men's views about pornography's encouragement of sexist and objectifying attitudes are corroborated by scholarship, finding that pornography consumption among adolescents is associated with more sexually objectifying and stereotypic gender views of women (Maes et al.,

2019; Peter & Valkenburg, 2007, 2009). For example, in an experimental study among young adults, pornography consumption was shown to increase notions of women as sex objects and to be associated with significantly stronger gender-stereotypic attitudes and cognitions (Hald et al., 2013). The young men featured in this book who expressed disquiet about pornography's effects in relationships also have grounds for concern, given the evidence that pornography consumption is associated with poorer relationship quality (Perry, 2020) and, in relation to joint pornography use among adolescent intimate partners, with lower skills in relationships and in refusing risky behaviours (Huntington et al., 2022).

A few of the young men raised concerns about how online pornography can distort young men's understanding of consent. Trevor (17, B, D) described the "whole porn industry" as "kind of warping the minds of what especially young men expect" and making it "a lot harder for people to understand consent online through like text and photos rather than if you're in person". Jesse (18, S) similarly noted that the absence of consent in pornography can contribute to a lack of understanding about what consent means in real-life situations: "like I don't think a lot of men understand it because they only, they just watch, and their idea of what consent is because there's no consent in porn and so they don't have that real concept of it". Ibrahim (18, S, CALD) expressed similar concerns. "in my experience, [it's] very toxic [in] how you view women". In his view, the ways in which women are represented in pornography, as submissive, appealed to "a lot of guys", as he explained:

> ...it's sad, but like [women are] obviously made to look like forced and that's what appeals to a lot of guys who do watch porn like is someone who's submissive and in a bad position. So, like to a lot of guys, it's very appealing and that's obviously what they [are] aiming for and they are acting but at the same time a lot of men don't know that. (Ibrahim, 18, S, CALD)

Again, such concerns are warranted. Pornography use is associated with attitudes supportive or tolerant of sexual aggression (Hald et al., 2010; Malamuth et al., 2012). Moreover, pornography use is associated with the actual perpetration of sexual violence. A meta-analysis—of 22 studies, from seven countries, comprising over 20,000 participants—finds consistent evidence that pornography consumption is associated with acts of sexual aggression, in both cross-sectional and longitudinal studies (Wright et al., 2015). Among young people, studies find associations between pornography use and the perpetration of teen dating violence (Rostad et al., 2019), online sexual solicitation and offline sexual harassment (Chang et al., 2016), sexual harassment (Kennair & Bendixen, 2012), and sexual violence (Bonino et al., 2006). Five longitudinal studies, including three among adolescents and teenagers, support the claim that pornography increases the likelihood that individuals will perpetrate sexual violence (Brown & L'Engle, 2009; D'Abreu & Krahé, 2014; Jongsma & Timmons Fritz, 2022; Waterman et al., 2022; Ybarra et al., 2011; Ybarra & Thompson, 2017). For example, in a recent longitudinal study of US middle and high school students over three years, young people who had viewed pornography were between 4.2 and 14.4 times more likely to go on to perpetrate sexual assault than young people who had not viewed pornography (Waterman et al., 2022). On the other hand, two longitudinal studies found no relationship between pornography use and subsequent perpetration of sexual aggression (Kohut et al., 2021) or intimate partner violence (Hatch et al., 2020).

Many of the young men expressed concerns about early exposure to online pornography. They pointed out that younger children, with more malleable brains, may perceive such content as normal due to its widespread availability. This early exposure was viewed as leading to distorted perceptions of what is normal, as Nate (18, S, CALD) commented: "I think the biggest thing is when you get younger kids who are on TikTok… what they see on the internet is perceived as all that's normal." Lleyton (16, S) commented on the prevalence of pornography online, "coming into younger generations" who "don't understand that it's merely like a movie, people act, and they sort of like take it the wrong way and they think it's real life and how it works". Jordan (16, S) expressed similar concerns about how younger generations compare pornography with their real-life experiences of sex and find the latter disappointing. Lucas (18, S) noted that "accessibility is a problem … you can literally just hop online and there's no kind of barriers … so I feel like it's allowed younger generations … to sort of access this material, which is probably horrible on [them]". Lucas (18, S) also commented on the dangers of desensitising children in relation to their early exposure to pornography as likely to lead to them experiencing "issues of intimacy … yeah, like I know people that have issues getting erect in terms of sex because [they are] so desensitised to it".

On the other hand, for a gay young man in this study, pornography helped him to understand gay male sexuality "a little bit better". Daniel (19, G) explained:

> … it was shown to me in school … I think I was 15 or something like that and then I didn't really go back into it until I was around 17. And then, you know, kind of discovered the whole gay thing and you know how that all worked and everything … I started [watching] straight porn when I was a kid, but yeah, it definitely helped in certain ways I suppose. Before I had seen gay porn … the only kind of attraction I had to guys was just pure attraction, it wasn't necessarily anything sexualised until yeah, I had seen it and then it just kind of, things made a lot more sense. Things became a lot more clear and yeah, I suppose it just changed my point of view … it was empowering to know who I was and understand things a little bit better. (Daniel, 19, G)

Particularly in a context where mainstream school-based sexuality education often says little about same-sex sexualities, pornography can be a particularly important means for young LGB people to learn about non-heterosexual sexual desires and practices (McCormack & Wignall, 2017). On the other hand, for gay and bisexual men pornography use also can intensify gender stereotypes, unrealistic body image standards (Benakovic et al., 2024), and preferences for and the practice of unsafe sex (Schrimshaw et al., 2016; Whitfield et al., 2018).

The concerns voiced by the young men in this section highlight the pervasive impact of online pornography on various facets of their lives (eSafety Commissioner, 2023). The ubiquity of explicit content on the internet poses a challenge in navigating online spaces for young men, with algorithms seemingly directing them towards adult material (eSafety Commissioner, 2023; 5Rights, 2021). To the extent that the young men in this research describe pornography as having negative impacts, they concur with most other young people in Australia. A survey of and focus groups among young people aged 16–18 found that two-thirds to three-quarters of young people felt that pornography had negative impacts on young people's understanding of consent (74%), ideas about intimate relationships (76%), expectations of sex (76%) and views on gender stereotypes (64%) (eSafety Commissioner, 2023).

The young men's comments illuminate some of the potential harms of early exposure to online pornography. The most prominent of these in their accounts involved struggles with addiction, with harmful impacts on mental health and relationships. Addiction also was a primary concern among boys in a New Zealand study (Meehan, 2023). This may reflect community and media focus on the harm of addiction rather than more feminist-informed critiques of pornography's role in patriarchal gender inequalities, as well the presence of websites such as 'Your Brain on Porn' and 'No Fap' communities in which men swear off masturbation (Dashiell & Rowland, 2024).

Narratives of 'addiction' have been criticised for resting on a distinction between normal and addictive pornography use, which both endorses pornography use *per se* as unproblematic and, for those who are 'addicted', excuses them from responsibility for their pornography consumption (Meehan, 2023). In such narratives, 'normal' pornography use is shielded from critique and its ethical and political ramifications are sidelined (Meehan, 2023; Taylor & Gavey, 2019). Rather than addressing how pornography and its users may harm women, attention is moved to how pornography may harm men. Nevertheless, although the young men in our study who noted pornography's potential harms emphasised addiction, they also acknowledged other forms of harm.

Many of the young men suggested that pornography fosters desensitisation and alters perceptions of women, distorting understandings of consent which reflects broader societal realities where sexual harassment, abuse and other forms of gender-based violence are highly prevalent. Such comments reflect a more critical response to pornography's content than some studies among young men have found (Antevska & Gavey, 2015). It is possible, however, that young men in our research with more positive attitudes towards pornography did not speak up, and it may have been harder to voice enthusiastic and potentially stigmatising views about pornography in this research's focus groups than in a one-on-one interview or anonymous survey. In the earlier Australian survey mentioned above, half of young people (51%) also thought that online pornography had some positive aspects, particularly in relation to learning about sex and exploring their sexuality (eSafety Commissioner, 2023).

Some participants in our research noted how the absence of representations of consent in pornography could contribute to a lack of understanding in offline/in-person situations. Young men emphasised the potential distortion of norms and expectations particularly among younger generations. Here, they show a similar pattern to the 'third person effect' evident in other research, in which young people position themselves as critical viewers of internet pornography while positioning other youth as at greater risk of being taken in by this material (Healy-Cullen et al., 2023).

The findings in this section highlight the young men's nuanced engagements with online pornography. Curatorial intentionality is evident in their attempts to filter and manage these experiences, rejecting or limiting exposure to sexually explicit content. However, their ability to fully control these encounters is undermined by algorithms that push adult material into their digital spaces, highlighting the limitations of personal agency in curating online experiences. Similarly, scepticism emerges as a significant critical disposition, with several young men expressing doubts about the authenticity of pornography, particularly regarding its portrayal of gender roles and relationships. Many critique the ways in which pornography distorts understandings of intimacy, consent, and women's agency, aligning with broader feminist critiques of the industry. However, despite this scepticism, some young men also acknowledge their own struggles with addiction-like consumption patterns, which complicates their ability to disengage from content they recognise as problematic.

These findings highlight the young men's ethical struggles with online pornography. What they understand to be important and good for themselves and others seems to inform their critical awareness of the negative impacts of pornography on theirs and others' lives—evident in their critique about pornography's ubiquity in their online lives, the 'battles' they have experienced with addiction, their views of pornography as unhealthy, shameful and regretful, their views of pornography as compromising their mental health, as objectifying women, as distorting their ideas of sexual consent and as degrading their relationships with intimate partners and girls/women. As with previous analyses, these ethical struggles extend to a concern with the impact of online pornography on younger generations, who are perceived as less able to navigate these harms. In relation to reflexivity, the young men's consideration of how pornography impacts on girls and women indicates a self-critical stance in relation to questioning and challenging their personal positionality (the gendered biases) shaping their consumption of online pornography.

Concerns with Commodifying and Sharing Intimate Images

The young men in this research expressed a range of opinions regarding the commodification and sharing of intimate images. In relation to image commodification, platforms such as OnlyFans (a content subscription service focused on pornography performers) were mentioned. Ibrahim (18, S, CALD) noted that those who could commodify their intimate lives online had found a way "to make money". While he noted that he didn't "necessarily agree with capitalism", he admired OnlyFan performers' capacity to capitalise on their content and make money through this avenue. Jordan's (16, S) perspective was that if people are willing to pay for intimate content on the OnlyFans site, there is no reason performers should not be able to earn "decent money" from it, "good for them". (Note that data on OnlyFans suggests that the large majority of women selling sexually explicit content on this platform make only small amounts of money from this.) Jordan suggested that some individuals may have had challenging life circumstances, and if this is a means for them to make a decent income then it is a valid choice.

Warren (18, S) also viewed this issue from a business perspective, recognising that these content creators have found a niche with high demand and low supply. He acknowledged the importance of these creators understanding that the money they earn may not last forever, especially as they age and their appearance changes. Nonetheless, Warren (18, S) spoke of respecting their ability to monetise their assets while they can.

These young men's relative comfort with this form of sex work is similar to that documented in other studies. In interviews with young people aged 12–16 in New Zealand, a small number of boys were concerned about the treatment of female performers, but they also dismissed this concern by offering individualist narratives of women's 'choice' to take part in pornography (Meehan, 2023, p. 85). Girls had more critical views of pornography, including expressing concern about the treatment of female performers and about the young female sexual partners of men who watch pornography (Meehan, 2023, pp. 52–53). Similarly, in a qualitative study among men in New Zealand, most aged in their early twenties, pornography users showed little concern for female performers and their wellbeing, including when they were shown engaged in or being subjected to physically demanding, degrading, and 'extreme' practices (Antevska & Gavey, 2015). More generally, compared to women, men have more accepting and positive attitudes towards sex work or transactional sex (Hansen & Johansson, 2022; Johansson & Hansen, 2024a Shamir et al., 2024, p. 300), and women associate sex work more strongly than men do with negative notions of poverty, women's exploitation, and human trafficking (Johansson & Hansen, 2024b). One complexity here is that people's attitudes towards sex work differ in relation to different practices in the 'whorearchy', with the sale of sex viewed less favourably and webcamming viewed more favourably (Puffer et al., 2024). Men's attitudes towards sex work also vary in association with their own willingness to consume or pay for sex (Puffer et al., 2024, p. 1181).

Ibrahim (18, S, CALD) raised an important concern about the vulnerability of individuals who attempt to monetise intimate content online. He highlighted the disparity between those who succeed in making money and those who don't, as he explained: "what we don't really know about is how many people try. How many people put that content out there that makes them vulnerable? All those people putting their content out there and not making any money off it … and then you know that stuff's online forever". He also expressed concern about the long-term consequences, both social and economic, of having such content available online. Ibrahim advocated for better education on the potential benefits and risks of engaging in this kind of work to ensure that individuals are fully informed before they make such decisions. He stressed the importance of preparing young men and women for the possible consequences and challenges they may face in the future due to their past involvement in online sex work.

Alongside the commercial production and sharing of sexual images and videos online on platforms such as OnlyFans, another practice is people's interpersonal sharing of sexual and intimate images with intimate partners and others. Sexting—the sharing of sexually explicit images, videos, and/or messages via electronic devices—is common among young adults, with a 2020 meta-analysis of 50 studies among 18-29 year-olds finding that 38.3% had sent sexts, 41.5% had received them, 47.7% had taken part in reciprocal sexting, and 15% had forwarded others' sexts without their consent (Mori et al., 2020).

The young men's perspectives on sharing intimate photos online resonated with other research among young men (Roberts & Ravn, 2019), finding a critical recognition of the potential harms of this practice as well as a significant emphasis on consent, mutuality and respect. In terms of potential harms, some of the young men acknowledged, for example, a stark gender disparity in how these images are perceived and received.

Nathan (17, S) highlighted this gendered dimension, noting that when it comes to leaked intimate photos, the consequences tend to be more severe for girls and women. He observed that while boys' leaked photos might result in some teasing, the intensity of the backlash faced by girls is notably higher, as he explained:

> ... let's take my school, for example, if there was a leak of a boy's photos ... people would probably laugh at it. It might be a bit of bullying, or just teasing for a while, but people generally get over it, but when it becomes like a female... it tends to be a lot more intense ... I would say it's more detrimental for a female than [for] a male. (Nathan, 17, S)

Sexist gender dynamics in relation to sexting and sexual imagery have been documented in a series of studies (Doyle et al., 2021; Dully et al., 2023; Waling et al., 2022). Patriarchal dynamics include pressure on girls and young women—directly, through coercion by male intimate partners and other males, and indirectly via social norms—to share sexual images, homosocial exchanges among boys and men of images of girls and women, 'slut shaming' responses to sexual images of girls and women, the harsher social scrutiny of and reputational damage among girls and women than boys and men when their images are shared or leaked, and the nonconsensual production or circulation of sexual images ('image based sexual abuse') particularly of girls and young women. Sexting thus reflects the gendered social relations visible among young people more generally.

In further reference to gender disparity, one of the young men commented on the different ways in which sharing intimate photos were received. Omer (17, S, CALD) commented,

> I'd be pretty happy [if I received an unsolicited pic] ... [if] a girl sends an unsolicited photo, a lot of guys are gonna start messaging that girl. Whereas if a guy is known for sending an unsolicited photo, that guy'll be known as a creep for the rest of his life. (Omer, 17, S, CALD)

The repercussions of sharing intimate photos online can be severe, as recounted by Jordan (16, S). He reflected on a personal experience where sharing intimate photos led to significant trouble, cautioning against such actions: "I did do it last year, but it's probably not something that I'd do again, I was pretty stupid. It just got me and this girl in a lot of trouble, and it wasn't worth it ... if your parents find it or something, you know, you just get in trouble". Omer (17, S, CALD) offered practical advice, suggesting that when sharing intimate photos, you should avoid showing your face so you can remain anonymous:

> … a pretty big incident, that my school wasn't aware of, but I think some girl in Year 10 sent … an intimate to a guy and that got screenshotted and then that was spread like wildfire. Number one [piece of advice] is probably just don't put your face in any [intimate photos]. (Omer, 17, S, CALD)

Miles (16, S) touched on the influence of age on the perception of receiving intimate photos: "I mean [receiving intimate photos] also kind of depends on … like age as well, if they're like the same age as you, it's better than someone who's like, 10-20 years older than you".

Many of the young men noted the significance of trust and caution when sharing intimate photos. Lucas (18, S) commented, "obviously trust plays a big part of it … I'm hesitant to do it [until I] definitely know I can trust that person." Toby (16, S) noted the importance of choosing the right person and the strength of the relationship when sharing intimate images: "I just think you have to be really careful when you do that … the type of relationship you have with that person, and can you really trust them" to not spread the photos around? He cautioned that a lack of discretion can lead to betrayal, recounting an incident where a male friend faced blackmail using such images following a breakup. Lleyton (16, S) similarly, stated:

> … you just gotta be really careful … cause it's so easy to spread these days and yeah, it [happened to] one of my friends. Someone sent him a few videos and he thought that he'd send one back and she took a screenshot and sent it everywhere. Yeah, it's crazy, but yeah, he put trust in her. She just broke it. (Lleyton, 16, S)

Other research finds similar emphases (Ravn & Roberts, 2019). For example, young heterosexual men in an Australian study who engaged in reciprocal sexting with intimate partners expressed concern about their sexual photos becoming public, with negative impacts on their future job prospects and families and a breaking of the implicit contract or trust involved (Waling et al., 2022). Although males are less vulnerable than females to reputational harm when their images are circulated, they too may face some risks.

The concept of online intimacy was met with mixed feelings. Eugene (19, S) expressed scepticism, finding it difficult to connect with the idea of online intimacy. He spoke of his preference for authenticity and the natural feel of in-person connections, as he explained:

> I feel like doing this sort of thing online is just not the same as doing it in real life … it feels really fake to be all intimate online … I feel like it's much more meaningful to do that in person … I'm a big advocate of things feeling natural. If it doesn't feel natural, I can't enjoy it at all. (Eugene, 19, S)

Similarly, Ari (19, S, CALD) expressed discomfort about "sending intimate photos" before meeting in person, stating, it's "not something I agree with, and I just feel like … there's no genuine connection there to do that kind of stuff … I just feel as though you're not connected physically so why should you physically show yourself online?" Kieran (19, S) also mentioned discomfort: "I wouldn't engage with [it] until there is a long-term relationship and, you know, with someone that I am really comfortable with. That level of intimacy is more with a future in mind". Jamie (16, First Nations) questioned the rationale behind unsolicited sharing, highlighting the judgment that often accompanies this practice. He stated:

> there's definitely a sort of a judgment, I guess, to someone sending that sort of stuff unsolicited because like you're not just gonna be in the middle of a conversation with someone and whip your tits out in the middle of the street. So why do you do it in the middle of a conversation on Instagram? (Jamie, 16, First Nations)

Daniel (19, G) offered a different perspective about online intimacy, noting that sharing intimate photos is "fairly normalised in the gay community", while Jamie (16, First Nations) expressed the view that sharing intimate photos "really depends a lot on how you see yourself". While he noted the significance of trust in sharing photos, he explained, "I've always been comfortable with my body, so I've definitely had my fair share of sending those sorts of photos … I've definitely always been a lot more open … I'm very proud of myself". These accounts echo those of young men in an Australian qualitative study of heterosexual cisgender men aged 18-30. When solicited between intimate partners, sexting, including the sending of 'dick pics', was a way to develop relationships, connection and intimacy, as well as a way to build confidence in a new relationship and a sense of desirability in themselves (Waling et al., 2022). At the same time, as the authors of that study comment, sending sexual images may involve less potential risks to males' sense of self and masculinity than sending messages expressing love and desire (Waling et al., 2022).

Some of the young men spoke about receiving unsolicited intimate images. Daniel (19, G) described receiving such images as "confronting", particularly when the sender is not of interest: "if you're not necessarily interested in that person or that kind of stuff, it can feel very confronting ... I suppose you just kind of ignore it and just move on considering how common it is, especially in the gay community". Kenneth (21, S) expressed mixed feelings, a blend of gratification and discomfort. He noted the exposure that comes with such content, especially when it arrives from someone with whom one has limited interaction. He commented:

> that's a very exposing way of being flattering if that makes sense. Yeah, especially to someone that you might have only met once, or might not have met at all ... but it's ... like, 'Well, okay, you sent one now here's the pressure for me to send one' ... and then it's like, if you don't send it, where do you go from there, right? Yeah, [I'm] pretty against it, to be honest. (Kenneth, 21, S)

These comments illustrate the young men's criticality and agency in relation to the commodifying and sharing of intimate images. As with previous sections, what seems to drive their concerns in this area are struggles relating to ethical engagement—what they conceive is important and good for themselves and others. For example, some of the young men admire the financial independence that content creators achieve selling sexually explicit material and they contextualise this commodification as positive for individual agency and financial gain. Others, however, note the vulnerability such commodifying brings, the risks associated with the permanency of sexualised online content and the gendered dimensions of sexual commodification where the negative consequences are far more pronounced for women than men (in terms of how this content is received). Many acknowledge that women face harsher scrutiny, reputational harm, and greater risks when their images are leaked, while men experience comparatively minimal social backlash. The young men's critical awareness of the gendered dimensions of sharing intimate content highlights a process of reflexivity, a questioning and challenging of the biases about gender that shape engagement. There is an implicit critique of the inequitable power imbalances in the digital sex economy.

Struggles for ethical engagement are also evident in the young men's personal views about online intimacy. They express concerns about disparities of age in the sharing of explicit content, and the trust and mutual respect requisite for them to personally share this content. The cautious engagement the young men advocate for intimate image-sharing and their tendency not to share these images are ethical moves which relate to what they understand to be important and good for themselves and others. These ethical moves are also about being responsible and accountable for actions that will have personal and relational impacts. These moves are productive for supporting gender justice (e.g., supporting trusting and mutually respectful gender relations). However, as noted in our earlier analyses, they represent an individualised focus on self-protection rather than broader discussions about how societal pressures, the gendered sex economy and the architectures of online spaces exploit and compound gender harms.

Concerns with Privacy and Safety Online

Many of the young men expressed concerns about their privacy and safety online. These concerns are not surprising given the predominance of protectionist discourses around online security in most facets of our social and working lives (Pangrazio, 2018). Drew (16, S, D, CALD), for example, raised concern about online scams, particularly directed at his parents, whom he was worried would fall victim to various fraudulent schemes. Manny (18, S) shared a personal story about his grandmother being scammed:

> I'm a little bit worried for my grandma to be honest, because last year she somehow fell for like one of those. I think it was a Nigerian prince who told her that he would give her lots of money, and he would come over and visit her, and she thought it was real which kind of made me realise that maybe they haven't been taught some of these things, and they don't realise how easy it is for the scam to kind of take control. (Manny, 18, S)

Leslie (17, S) also noted his concerns about older people's vulnerability to scams, recounting an incident of a friend's grandmother losing thousands of dollars to an international scammer.

Henry (16, S) noted that "everyone should be somewhat concerned" with issues of privacy online. As he stated, "most websites or platforms nowadays do track what you're doing a lot of the time" and we don't really know "what's happening with that information". Theo (18, S, A) highlighted the importance of safeguarding personal information online to protect against potential harassment or threats because he had been subject to trolling, so he took measures to "keep [his] private information private", while Majak (21, S, CALD) noted encountering scams on platforms like Facebook Marketplace associated with buying a car and the need for vigilance to avoid falling victim to such schemes.

Some of the young men commented on their experiences of 'catfishing' (the use of fictitious online personas or identities to deceive) and impersonation. Daniel (19, G) discussed instances of catfishing on Grindr (a gay dating app) and Instagram, emphasising how the misuse of personal information and identity theft can be unsettling, as he explained:

> There's been a few times where, you know, catfishing is such a huge thing when it comes to social media … I've had my photos used before as well online, so people have used [them] to create accounts, a few on Grindr, a few on Instagram which can be quite unsettling, especially when people are like, 'Oh, you know, is this you? Like what's going on?' And it's all just a bit confronting … I suppose it's all so fake. You don't really see much of anyone so it honestly could be absolutely anyone that's behind that screen … it was, I mean. Look, there's a hint of flattery, let's face it but … [and] then obviously, you've kind of got to [tell] people, to be like, "Look, not me", awkward. (Daniel, 19, G)

Practices of deception and fraud are common in online dating. For example, recent reviews find that substantial proportions of social media users have been subject to online romance fraud and that victims are more likely to be women than men (Bilz et al., 2023; Coluccia et al., 2020). At the same time, dating sites include deceptive profiles targeting men as well as women, and there has been a recent increase in sextortion attempts aimed at young men (Bilz et al., 2023).

Elliott (21, Prefer not to say) also described cases of impersonation, where individuals had created fake profiles using his name and images, "so I've got like two random Instagram accounts with my name and face that don't belong to me, and I have no reason. I don't know why they do it". Kenneth (21, S) similarly described an experience of impersonation on a dating site he had never used: "I've never got into the whole online dating thing, but a lot of my friends have … one of my friends showed me a profile that was one of my photos [and] I've never been on it. That's super weird".

For several of the young men, the risk of potential breaches of privacy led to conscious action to limit their digital presence. Lee (18, S, CALD), Omer (17, S, CALD) and Vish (20, S, CALD) emphasised their efforts to limit their digital footprints, with Lee noting "I don't share photos of myself online to make sure that if there's any predators, they don't know who I am"; Omer (17, S, CALD) described being cautious about revealing personal information: "I don't put my name in any of my socials except for Facebook … yeah, I try to keep my digital footprint as low as possible". Vish (20, S, CALD) ensures that his account "is private so like no one can view any of my stuff if they're not already accepted into my following list". He added, "I rarely post or share anything that is revealing like even if it's to my friends. I take that level of like privacy as well like not share my face or like any details about like where I have like locations or stuff just [for] like [an] extra layer of security".

Vincent (21, S) expressed concerns about the tracking of online activities by various platforms. He spoke of taking care about what he posted online that might be accessible to a "future employer". Geoffrey (20, G, CALD) discussed the importance of minimising his digital footprint due to concerns about personal safety and privacy, as he explained:

> I think that it's very crazy how quickly you can leave a digital footprint. And the more I think about it, the more I'm keen to avoid leaving a massive digital footprint for a number of reasons. There's people tracking people down and stuff and, you know, but also just even for my work, for practical reasons like the work that I do, it's not really good to have public attention so for a number of reasons and I think privacy is such a big thing now and there's all like these hackings and like you know information scandals and so I think there's lots of reasons to be like very privacy conscious. (Geoffrey, 20, G, CALD)

Similarly, Nathan (17, S) spoke of the potential damage to your image "in other people's minds" when compromising "personal information" is leaked "in an uncontrolled sense", as he explained:

> … say, a private photo of me [is leaked] like I'm trying to build a rep [reputation] at the minute with sort of professional theatre … it's career ending and if you're trying to get into a prestigious college or university, or a job and you've got a history where that's been leaked and it's completely out of

> your control. It's damaging. It really is. I think, for a number of reasons. The biggest one, obviously, is that a level of intimacy and privacy of your life is now just public … but also in a sense of there's a question of control there, and the people who you trust, and where you're sending your material and stuff that can lead to people questioning the authenticity of you, in a sense, yeah, like, is it really you? (Nathan, 17, S)

Vish (20, S, CALD) spoke of taking similar precautions: "I guess it's just a personal preference, but I mean, like in the past my personal stuff has been leaked before so [I take as] many precautions that I can … [so] now I make sure I go through, like anyone who requests to follow me, I do background checks on background checks". Phil (16, S) in contrast, noted that he didn't "worry too much about safety and privacy simply because my entire presence online is almost like zero percent personal".

In general, men tend to take fewer steps than women to protect their privacy online, as a 2019 meta-analysis documents (Tifferet, 2019). They show greater risk-taking attitudes and are more likely to share personal information on social networking sites compared to women (Fogel & Nehmad, 2009). An early UK study finds that male adolescents tend to be less safety-aware online than females, possibly due to societal norms and female-targeted safety campaigns (Pedersen, 2013), and indeed, cybersafety campaigns often have focused particularly on girls' vulnerability to exploitation and responsibility for avoiding this (Brand, 2016).

However, the popular stereotype of young people as cavalier about their online privacy is false. Young adults are often at least as concerned (Hoofnagle et al., 2010) or more concerned about privacy than older generations (Blank et al., 2014). Research among US older teens finds that they are concerned about their online privacy, particularly at the prospect of unintended audiences seeing their personal information, although they feel pressure to share personal information among friends, but they are less concerned about safety, tending to feel safe online and to employ protective measures (Agosto & Abbas, 2017). In a US study among young adults aged 19–35, while respondents engaged in some privacy-protective behaviours, many also felt a lack of control over shared information due to institutional practices and technological affordances (Hargittai & Marwick, 2016).

Another area of concern raised by the young men in relation to online safety was regulation and censorship. Campbell (18, B, D) and Chen (18, G, CALD) both grappled with the idea of censorship, acknowledging that while some moderation may be necessary, excessive censorship can limit perspectives and access to important information, as they explained:

> I feel like on TikTok and stuff, some of the content I see I know isn't moderated for younger audiences because I feel like some of the stuff that a lot of younger audiences see … I don't think that they should be able to. (Campbell, 18, B, D)

> Like there is a certain degree where stuff should be censored but you can also say that if you just censor everything, that is negative. For example, like, let's say about like just world crisis. If you censor out all the worldly crisis in the world, you yourself would not have a good understanding of what's actually happening in the world, which kind of limits your perspective. (Chen, 18, G, CALD)

Jamie (16, First Nations) pointed out the complexity of regulating the internet, making it challenging to find a one-size-fits-all solution, while Jordan (16, S), like Campbell (18, B, D), advocated for increased regulation, especially regarding online content accessibility to younger people: "basically everything [is] super easy nowadays and, you know, that's really not good for kids, our age or anyone really so I think you know [we need] more regulation and rules around it". Spencer (18, B, CALD) similarly noted, "I would make it ten times safer … especially, kids" to curb "the dangers [for] them [on the] internet … you want to have some control about what they're gonna see", while Benito (20, S, CALD) advocated "moderation" for "dangerous" platforms like Twitter (X) "to filter out certain things" but noted that "most social medias have pretty good sort of limits as to what you can consume".

Benito (20, S, CALD) and Tristan (18, S) discussed the importance of individual responsibility in managing exposure to online content, citing platform features that allow users to control their experiences:

> I think people have different things that would trigger them in terms of content being harmful to them so I think to an extent, it's a bit of their responsibility to sort of limit as much content that they take in … most social media apps at the moment have a fair bit of like security in terms of turning off things or limiting things … the app itself like Instagram has a lot of like warnings and things like that where it'll come up saying like this content is unreliable or maybe edited and things like that so I think when it comes down to that, it's sort of, there are ways to navigate around it. (Benito, 20, S, CALD)

US data find that teenagers place greater emphasis than older people on the importance of people being able to feel welcome and safe online over the importance of people being able to speak their minds freely online. On the other hand, among both young people and older adults, females are more likely than males to prioritise feeling welcome and safe and to say offensive content is too often excused (Pew Research Center, 2022). Similarly, national UK data find that women are more at risk than men of being targeted by harms including online misogyny, cyberstalking and cyberflashing, are significantly more fearful of being targeted by harms overall, report greater negative psychological impacts, report higher use of a range of safety tools, and are less comfortable with various forms of online participation (Enock et al., 2024).

In this section, the young men's scepticism, curatorial intentionality, ethical engagement and reflexivity are evident in their recognition and questioning of the harms and dangers produced by online architectures and relationships. In response to these potential dangers, they exercise scepticism and caution in their sharing of information, e.g. to avoid catfishing and impersonation. Their curatorial intentionality is evident in their conscious actions to limit their digital footprint by restricting personal information on social media, avoiding online self-presentation, and employing privacy settings. These practices reflect an understanding of digital self-curation as a means of safeguarding their online identity and mitigating risks (e.g., relating to the sharing of information that might compromise future employment) and are reflexive in their consideration of the long-term implications of digital exposure for relationships, reputations and careers.

Of prominence in this section, as with earlier analyses, are the young men's ethical struggles with privacy and safety online. These struggles are clear in the ongoing tensions they express about what is important and good for themselves and others. Their criticisms of online scams, identity theft and the misuse of personal information indicate concerns about the unethical ways that online spaces seek to engage people. Further ethical concerns were expressed in relation to regulation and censorship, with some advocating for greater regulation of negative online content and others questioning such regulation. Such struggles indicate the young men's capacities to question and resist digital interactions and structures that are exploitative and harmful. However, their remedies put forth for mitigating these harms are again focused on personal responsibility and individual actions for self-protection—which abdicates responsibility for better management of digital privacy among policymakers and technologies companies.

Conclusion

This chapter has highlighted young men's concerns about sex, intimacy, and privacy in online spaces. Their largely negative reflections on pornography were associated with its ubiquity online, its distortion of sexual consent, and its objectification of women. Curatorial intentionality, scepticism, ethical engagement, and reflexivity were evident in the young men's efforts to manage their exposure. However, these efforts were often framed through individual struggles with self-control rather than through recognition of broader gendered harms. The young men also expressed concerns about the sharing of intimate images, noting the different gendered expectations and higher reputational costs of sexting for girls and women and the importance of mutual trust when engaging in this practice. Their anxieties about privacy and safety were related to scams, catfishing, and digital footprints, again understood primarily in terms of personal responsibility for self-protection. The next chapter draws together the findings and insights from the research to highlight the significance of fostering young men's critical digital dispositions for gender justice.

References

5Rights. (2021). *Pathways: How digital design puts children at risk.* https://5rightsfoundation.com/uploads/Pathways-how-digital-design-puts-children-at-risk.pdf

Agosto, D. E., & Abbas, J. (2017). "Don't be dumb—That's the rule I try to live by": A closer look at older teens' online privacy and safety attitudes. *New Media & Society, 19*(3), 347–365.

Antevska, A., & Gavey, N. (2015). "Out of sight and out of mind": Detachment and men's consumption of male sexual dominance and female submission in pornography. *Men and Masculinities, 18*(5), 605–629.

Benakovic, R., Wilson, M. J., & Seidler, Z. (2024). Pleasure and peril: Young men's mental health in the world of porn. In Z. Seidler (Ed.), *Masculinities and mental health in young men: From echo chambers to evidence* (pp. 263–312). Springer.

Bilz, A., Shepherd, L. A., & Johnson, G. I. (2023). Tainted love: A systematic literature review of online romance scam research. *Interacting with Computers, 35*(6), 773–788.

Blank, G., Bolsover, G., & Dubois, E. (2014). A new privacy paradox: Young people and privacy on social network sites. *Prepared for the annual meeting of the American Sociological Association*, 17 August 2014, San Francisco, CA. https://ssrn.com/abstract=2479938 or https://doi.org/10.2139/ssrn.2479938.

Bonino, S., Ciairano, S., Rabaglietti, E., & Cattelino, E. (2006). Use of pornography and self-reported engagement in sexual violence among adolescents. *European Journal of Developmental Psychology, 3*(3), 265–288.

Brand, C. (2016). *"Make smart choices!": Discourses of girlhood responsibilization in cybersafety curricula*. (Unpublished masters thesis). University of Victoria.

Brown, J. D., & L'Engle, K. L. (2009). X-rated: Sexual attitudes and behaviors associated with US early adolescents' exposure to sexually explicit media. *Communication Research, 36*(1), 129–151.

Carroll, J. S., Padilla-Walker, L. M., Nelson, L. J., Olson, C. D., McNamara Barry, C., & Madsen, S. D. (2008). Generation XXX: Pornography acceptance and use among emerging adults. *Journal of Adolescent Research, 23*(1), 6–30.

Chang, F. C., Chiu, C. H., Miao, N. F., Chen, P. H., Lee, C. M., & Chiang, J. T. (2016). Predictors of unwanted exposure to online pornography and online sexual solicitation of youth. *Journal of Health Psychology, 21*(6), 1107–1118.

Coluccia, A., Pozza, A., Ferretti, F., Carabellese, F., Masti, A., & Gualtieri, G. (2020). Online romance scams: Relational dynamics and psychological characteristics of the victims and scammers. A scoping review. *Clinical Practice and Epidemiology in Mental Health: CP & EMH, 16*, 24.

Crabbe, M., Flood, M., & Adams, K. (2024). Pornography exposure and access among young Australians: A cross-sectional study. *Australian and New Zealand Journal of Public Health, 48*, 100135.

D'Abreu, L. C. F., & Krahé, B. (2014). Predicting sexual aggression in male college students in Brazil. *Psychology of Men & Masculinity, 15*(2), 152.

Dashiell, S., & Rowland, A. (2024). Erotic habitus and collapsed masculinity in male-dominated spaces: The case of the no Fap relapse spaces. *Sexualities*, 13634607241230748. https://doi.org/10.1177/13634607241230748

Davis, A., Carrotte, E., Hellard, M., Temple-Smith, M., & Lim, M. (2017). "I think it has been a negative influence in many ways but at the same time I can't stop using it": Self-identified problematic pornography use among a sample of young Australians. *Sexually Transmitted Infections, 93*(Suppl 2), A195–A196. http://sti.bmj.com/content/93/Suppl_2/A195.3.abstract

de Alarcón, R., de la Iglesia, J. I., Casado, N. M., & Montejo, A. L. (2019). Online porn addiction: What we know and what we don't—A systematic review. *Journal of Clinical Medicine, 8*(1), 91.

Doyle, C., Douglas, E., & O'Reilly, G. (2021). The outcomes of sexting for children and adolescents: A systematic review of the literature. *Journal of Adolescence, 92*, 86–113.

Dully, J., Walsh, K., Doyle, C., & O'Reilly, G. (2023). Adolescent experiences of sexting: A systematic review of the qualitative literature, and recommendations for practice. *Journal of Adolescence, 95*(6), 1077–1105.

Dwulit, A. D., & Rzymski, P. (2019). The potential associations of pornography use with sexual dysfunctions: An integrative literature review of observational studies. *Journal of Clinical Medicine, 8*(7), 914.

Enock, F. E., Stevens, F., Bright, J., Cross, M., Johansson, P., Wajcman, J., & Margetts, H. Z. (2024). Understanding gender differences in experiences and concerns surrounding online harms: A short report on a nationally representative survey of UK adults. *Computer Science, Computer and Society, arXiv preprint arXiv:2402.00463.*

eSafety Commissioner. (2023). *Accidental, unsolicited and in your face: Young people's encounters with online pornography: A matter of platform responsibility, education and choice.* https://apo.org.au/node/324428

Fogel, J., & Nehmad, E. (2009). Internet social network communities: Risk taking, trust, and privacy concerns. *Computers in Human Behavior, 25*(1), 153–160.

Grubbs, J. B., & Gola, M. (2019). Is pornography use related to erectile functioning? Results from cross-sectional and latent growth curve analyses. *The Journal of Sexual Medicine, 16*(1), 111–125.

Hald, G. M., Malamuth, N. M., & Yuen, C. (2010). Pornography and attitudes supporting violence against women: Revisiting the relationship in nonexperimental studies. *Aggressive Behavior, 36*(1), 14–20.

Hald, G. M., Malamuth, N. N., & Lange, T. (2013). Pornography and sexist attitudes among heterosexuals. *Journal of Communication, 63*(4), 638–660.

Hansen, M. A., & Johansson, I. (2022). Predicting attitudes towards transactional sex: The interactive relationship between gender and attitudes on sexual behaviour. *Sexuality Research & Social Policy, 19*, 1–14.

Hargittai, E., & Marwick, A. (2016). "What can I really do?": Explaining the privacy paradox with online apathy. *International Journal of Communication, 10*(21), 3737–3757.

Hatch, S. G., Esplin, C. R., Aaron, S. C., Dowdle, K. K., Fincham, F. D., Hatch, H. D., & Braithwaite, S. R. (2020). Does pornography consumption lead to intimate partner violence perpetration? Little evidence for temporal precedence. *The Canadian Journal of Human Sexuality, 29*(3), 289–296.

Healy-Cullen, S., Morison, T., Taylor, J. E., & Taylor, K. (2023). What does it mean to be 'porn literate': Perspectives of young people, parents and teachers in Aotearoa New Zealand. *Culture, Health & Sexuality, 26*, 1–17. https://doi.org/10.1080/13691058.2023.2194355

Hoofnagle, C. J., King, J., Li, S., & Turow, J. (2010). How different are young adults from older adults when it comes to information privacy attitudes and policies?. Available at SSRN 1589864.

Huntington, C., Willoughby, B., & Rhoades, G. (2022). Associations of adolescents' pornography viewing with their romantic relationship skills and behaviors. *The Journal of Sex Research, 61*, 1–12.

Jacobs, T., Geysemans, B., Van Hal, G., Glazemakers, I., Fog-Poulsen, K., Vermandel, A., De Wachter, S., & De Win, G. (2021). Associations between online pornography consumption and sexual dysfunction in young men: Multivariate analysis based on an international web-based survey. *JMIR Public Health and Surveillance, 7*(10), e32542.

Johansson, I., & Hansen, M. A. (2024a). Predicting attitudes towards the exchange of sexual services for payment: Variance in gender gaps across the Nordic countries. *Sexuality Research & Social Policy, 21*, 1–19.

Johansson, I., & Hansen, M. A. (2024b). From empowerment to exploitation: Predicting positive and negative associations with the exchange of sexual services for payment. *Sexuality & Culture, 28*(3), 1184–1206.

Jongsma, K., & Timmons Fritz, P. (2022). The role of pornography use in intimate partner violence in different-sex couples: A prospective longitudinal study. *Journal of Interpersonal Violence, 37*(21–22), NP20873–NP20897.

Kennair, L. E. O., & Bendixen, M. (2012). Sociosexuality as predictor of sexual harassment and coercion in female and male high school students. *Evolution and Human Behavior, 33*(5), 479–490.

Kohut, T., Landripet, I., & Štulhofer, A. (2021). Testing the confluence model of the association between pornography use and male sexual aggression: A longitudinal assessment in two independent adolescent samples from Croatia. *Archives of Sexual Behavior, 50*(2), 647–665.

Landripet, I., & Štulhofer, A. (2015). Is pornography use associated with sexual difficulties and dysfunctions among younger heterosexual men? *The Journal of Sexual Medicine, 12*(5), 1136–1139.

Lim, M. S., Agius, P. A., Carrotte, E. R., Vella, A. M., & Hellard, M. E. (2017). Young Australians' use of pornography and associations with sexual risk behaviours. *Australian and New Zealand Journal of Public Health, 41*(4), 438–443.

Löfgren-Mårtenson, L., & Månsson, S.-A. (2010). Lust, love, and life: A qualitative study of Swedish adolescents' perceptions and experiences with pornography. *Journal of Sex Research, 47*(6), 568–579.

Love, T., Laier, C., Brand, M., Hatch, L., & Hajela, R. (2015). Neuroscience of internet pornography addiction: A review and update. *Behavioral Sciences, 5*(3), 388.

Maes, C., Schreurs, L., van Oosten, J. M. F., & Vandenbosch, L. (2019). #(Me) too much? The role of sexualizing online media in adolescents' resistance towards the metoo-movement and acceptance of rape myths. *Journal of Adolescence, 77*, 59–69.

Malamuth, N. M., Hald, G. M., & Koss, M. (2012). Pornography, individual differences in risk and men's acceptance of violence against women in a representative sample. *Sex Roles, 66*(7–8), 427–439.

Martellozzo, E., Monaghan, A., Adler, J. R., Davidson, J., Leyva, R., & Horvath, M. A. (2016). *"I wasn't sure it was normal to watch it…" A quantitative and qualitative examination of the impact of online pornography on the values, attitudes, beliefs and behaviours of children and young people.* Middlesex University, NSPCC, OCC.

McCormack, M., & Wignall, L. (2017). Enjoyment, exploration and education: Understanding the consumption of pornography among young men with non-exclusive sexual orientations. *Sociology, 51*(5), 975–991.

Meehan, C. (2023). *The politics of porn for young people in New Zealand.* Springer.

Mori, C., Cooke, J. E., Temple, J. R., Ly, A., Lu, Y., Anderson, N., Rash, C., & Madigan, S. (2020). The prevalence of sexting behaviors among emerging adults: A meta-analysis. *Archives of Sexual Behavior, 49*(4), 1103–1119.

Pangrazio, L. (2018). *Young people's literacies in the digital age: Continuities, conflicts and contradictions.* Routledge.

Park, B. Y., Wilson, G., Berger, J., Christman, M., Reina, B., Bishop, F., Klam, W. P., & Doan, A. P. (2016). Is internet pornography causing sexual dysfunctions? A review with clinical reports. *Behavioral Sciences, 6*(3), 17.

Pedersen, S. (2013). UK young adults' safety awareness online—Is it a 'girl thing'? *Journal of Youth Studies, 16*(3), 404–419.

Perry, S. L. (2020). Pornography and relationship quality: Establishing the dominant pattern by examining pornography use and 31 measures of relationship quality in 30 national surveys. *Archives of Sexual Behavior, 49*(4), 1199–1213.

Peter, J., & Valkenburg, P. M. (2007). Adolescents' exposure to a sexualized media environment and their notions of women as sex objects. *Sex Roles, 56*(5–6), 381.

Peter, J., & Valkenburg, P. M. (2009). Adolescents' exposure to sexually explicit internet material and notions of women as sex objects: Assessing causality and underlying processes. *Journal of Communication, 59*(3), 407–433.

Pew Research Center. (2022, August 30). *More so than adults, U.S. teens value people feeling safe online over being able to speak freely.* Pew Research Center. https://www.pewresearch.org/short-reads/2022/08/30/more-so-than-adults-u-s-teens-value-people-feeling-safe-online-over-being-able-to-speak-freely/

Puffer, H., Hodson, G., & Prusaczyk, E. (2024). Attitudes toward cisgender women's participation in sex work: Opportunity for agency or harmful exchange? *Archives of Sexual Behavior, 53*(3), 1169–1185.

Ravn, S., & Roberts, S. (2019). Young masculinities: Masculinities in youth studies. In L. Gottzén, U. Mellström, & T. Shefer (Eds.), *Routledge international handbook of masculinity studies* (pp. 183–191). Routledge.

Rissel, C., Richters, J., de Visser, R. O., McKee, A., Yeung, A., & Caruana, T. (2017). A profile of pornography users in Australia: Findings from the second Australian study of health and relationships. *The Journal of Sex Research, 54*(2), 227–240.

Roberts, S., & Ravn, S. (2019). Towards a sociological understanding of sexting as a social practice: A case study of university undergraduate men. *Sociology, 54*(2), 258–274.

Rostad, W. L., Gittins-Stone, D., Huntington, C., Rizzo, C. J., Pearlman, D., & Orchowski, L. (2019). The association between exposure to violent pornography and teen dating violence in grade 10 high school students. *Archives of Sexual Behavior, 48*, 1–11.

Schrimshaw, E. W., Antebi-Gruszka, N., & Downing, M. J., Jr. (2016). Viewing of internet-based sexually explicit media as a risk factor for condomless anal sex among men who have sex with men in four US cities. *PLoS ONE, 11*(4), e0154439.

Shamir, H., Peled, E., & Shilo, G. (2024). Predictors of public attitudes regarding the impact of "end demand" legislation: Findings from an Israeli survey. *Sexuality Research & Social Policy, 21*(1), 297–312.

Taylor, K., & Gavey, N. (2019). Pornography addiction and the perimeters of acceptable pornography viewing. *Sexualities, 23*(5 6), 876 897. https://doi.org/10.1177/1363460719861826

Tifferet, S. (2019). Gender differences in privacy tendencies on social network sites: A meta-analysis. *Computers in Human Behavior, 93*, 1–12. https://doi.org/10.1016/j.chb.2018.11.046

Waling, A., Kerr, L., Bourne, A., Power, J., & Kehler, M. (2022). 'It's nice to be appreciated': Understanding heterosexual men's engagements with sexting and sharing dick pics. *Sexualities, 25*(3), 198–221. https://doi.org/10.1177/1363460720947297

Waterman, E. A., Wesche, R., Morris, G., Edwards, K. M., & Banyard, V. L. (2022). Prospective associations between pornography viewing and sexual aggression among adolescents. *Journal of Research on Adolescence*. https://doi.org/10.1111/jora.12745

Whitfield, T. H., Rendina, H. J., Grov, C., & Parsons, J. T. (2018). Sexually explicit media and condomless anal sex among gay and bisexual men. *AIDS and Behavior, 22*(2), 681–689.

Wright, P. J., Sun, C., Steffen, N. J., & Tokunaga, R. S. (2015). Pornography, alcohol, and male sexual dominance. *Communication Monographs, 82*(2), 252–270.

Ybarra, M. L., Mitchell, K. J., Hamburger, M., Diener-West, M., & Leaf, P. J. (2011). X-rated material and perpetration of sexually aggressive behavior among children and adolescents: Is there a link? *Aggressive Behavior, 37*(1), 1–18.

Ybarra, M. L., & Thompson, R. E. (2017). Predicting the emergence of sexual violence in adolescence. *Prevention Science, 19*(4), 403–415. https://doi.org/10.1007/s11121-017-0810-4

CHAPTER 6

Cultivating Critical Digital Dispositions for Gender Justice

Abstract This chapter draws together the findings and insights from the research to highlight the significance of fostering young men's critical digital dispositions for gender justice. This involves supporting young men to interrogate the digital cultures that promote rigid ideas and enactments of gender and masculinity towards creating more equitable and gender just digital spaces. The first part of the chapter considers the study's findings in relation to a gender justice framing of the four critical digital dispositions informing the book's analysis: curatorial intentionality, scepticism, ethical engagement and reflexivity. It articulates how the young men's online engagements both support and hinder gender justice—i.e., how their online encounters challenge *and* reproduce restrictive and harmful gendered norms. The second part of the chapter provides a series of activity ideas aimed at strengthening these gender justice or feminist-aligned dispositions. The final section of this chapter recognises the need for broader action on the part of policymakers and technology companies working together to create better frameworks that protect individuals from harm and foster ethical online behaviour.

Keywords Young men • Critical digital dispositions • Curatorial intentionality • Scepticism • Ethical engagement • Reflexivity • Gender justice

A. Keddie, M. Flood, *Young Men's Online Lives*,
https://doi.org/10.1007/978-3-031-99980-2_6

A Gender Justice Framing of the Four Critical Digital Dispositions

As argued in Chapter 1, the four critical digital dispositions offered in Pangrazio's work (2018) provide a powerful and comprehensive lens for understanding how young men are engaging critically with their online experiences. When combined with a gender justice framing, they draw attention to the ways in which young men's engagements can both challenge and reinforce harmful gender norms. Bringing gender justice into view provides rich insight into how the dispositions of curatorial intentionality, scepticism, ethical engagement, and reflexivity can disrupt harmful gendered digital cultures. This framing also, importantly, illuminates the limitations of the young men's engagements—highlighting, for example, how they tend not to extend their critical engagement beyond an individual and personal level of navigation, management and responsibility. The following sections consider each of the four dispositions through a gender justice lens, illustrating how they might be directed towards more inclusive and equitable online cultures.

Curatorial Intentionality and Gender Justice

As noted in Chap. 1, curatorial intentionality is defined in this book as the deliberate and intentional process of navigating, filtering and selecting online content to align with particular wants, needs, values and purposes. It represents the capacity to curate the self in ways that are sensitive to the affordances and audiences of different platforms (Pangrazio, 2018; Weinstein & James, 2022). Intentionality in the process of curating content to consume or create is an act of agency and a willingness to engage with, and potentially transform, dominant social discourses (Stenalt, 2021). In relation to gender justice, curatorial intentionality would be evident in young men's critical awareness of the equity implications involved in their navigation, filtering and selection of content to consume and create—e.g., the extent to which such intentionality challenges or reproduces restrictive and harmful gendered norms.

In relation to leisure, work and identity (Chap. 2), the young men demonstrated curatorial intentionality in their purposeful and strategic engagement with digital platforms such as TikTok, YouTube, WhatsApp, and Discord (curating content and tools to align with their interests, aspirations and values) and in their attempts to moderate their over-use of these media through employing app blockers or deleting applications to regain control over their screen time. In this chapter we noted a conflict between these efforts of curatorial intentionality and the platform mechanics such as infinite scrolling and algorithmic content loops, that undermine them. We also noted how individual agency framed the young men's curatorial intentionality—as a personal responsibility of self-control rather than the responsibility of online platforms.

Curatorial intentionality in this chapter was also evident in the young men's selective engagements with self-improvement and male empowerment content and their deliberate management of their online identities and self-presentation for different audiences. This is where the gendered dimensions of curatorial intentionality became apparent. Regarding self-improvement, the young men shared mixed feelings about the male empowerment messages promoted by social media influencer Andrew Tate, with some endorsing his male empowerment narratives as speaking out for men in a world where feminism has taken over and others critiquing the narrow versions of masculinity promoted by Tate. While the former led to a curating of content to include Tate (reproducing restrictive and harmful gender norms), the latter led to a curation excluding Tate (rejecting his harmful gender norms). Young men's engagement with body image standards and social media posting similarly varied: some rejected the pressures of social media comparisons and positioned posting as a feminine act, while others critiqued the gendered double standards affecting women's online self-presentation. These views led to an avoidance of posting. We noted here the broader discourses of masculinity as invulnerable as shaping the young men's reluctance to post, and the pressures they encounter to curate themselves to conform to unrealistic masculine body standards and to compete with others in relation to these and other life standards. These practices reproduce binary understandings of gender as difference and opposition.

In Chap. 3 which explored connection, community and conflict, the young men's curatorial intentionality was evident in their deliberate engagements with the affordances of digital communities (and platforms such as Snapchat, Instagram, Facebook, and Discord) to meet their needs for social and emotional connection and support. This curation disrupts the stoicism, emotional detachment, and aversion to vulnerability associated with restrictive and harmful masculine norms. However, the young men's curatorial intentionality within other online spaces—especially gaming environments—was a different story. The relational and contextual dynamics in these environments, encouraged by algorithms and platform mechanics designed to amplify competition and abuse, fuelled hostility.

Here the young men's curation to engage in male-dominated online environments reinforced restrictive gender norms and limited their exposure to diverse perspectives. Additionally, the young men's curation of online spaces to avoid toxicity (evident in their selective disengagement from divisive discussions) was thwarted by platform architectures that pulled them back into polarising content and hostile debates.

Curatorial intentionality was further evident in the young men's critical awareness of how algorithms shape their online experiences, how they can amplify harmful and extreme content, how they can create echo chambers, and how they are designed to keep them engaged for long periods (Chap. 4). This critical awareness of algorithms shaped the young men's content curation. However, it did not tend to focus on gender. While there was some recognition of algorithms targeting their demographics as young men and leading them to masculinised and sexist content, this recognition was rare. The young men's approach to misinformation in this chapter further illustrated curatorial intentionality. Their curation was informed by their awareness of and attempts to navigate misinformation and the need to distinguish between credible and false information. Again, Andrew Tate was a point of discussion, with curatorial intentionality shaped here by beliefs about misrepresentation. Those young men who curated their online experiences to include content produced by Andrew Tate defended him on the basis that his views are misrepresented (i.e., taken out of context and distorted). Such defence reinforces the legitimacy of Tate's messages of misogyny and sexism.

In relation to matters of sex, intimacy, and privacy (Chap. 5), the young men's curatorial intentionality shaped their engagement with online pornography and digital sexual economies. Such curation was driven by their concerns that explicit content is too ubiquitous and accessible in their lives, as addictive, as objectifying and degrading of women, as distorting ideas of sexual consent and as dulling their emotional reactions to explicit content. These negative views led to the young men's efforts to filter and manage their exposure to pornography, efforts that can be seen as challenging and seeking to transform harmful gender norms. However, such attempts were undermined by the algorithms pushing adult content into their digital spaces and the onus placed on young men to be responsible for managing these algorithms. Similarly, curatorial intentionality in this chapter shaped the young men's sharing of intimate images: their critical recognition of the potential harms of sharing intimate images shaped their decisions about sharing and their views that caution and trust are central to making these decisions. This, and some of the young men's recognition of the gender disparities of sharing (i.e., that young women face harsher scrutiny and reputational harm than men if sharing sexually explicit images of themselves), indicate a challenging of gendered norms that position young men as uncaring or uncritical in this space. Finally, this chapter examined the young men's views about digital privacy and their curatorial intentionality towards self-protection (e.g., limiting digital presence and being cautious about what they share). However, again, responsibility for such protection is individualised—the young men take responsibility to manage risks to security and privacy.

Scepticism and Gender Justice

As described in Chap. 1, scepticism is conceptualised in this book as questioning the assumptions and biases embedded in online content including the architectures (e.g., platform affordances and algorithms) that encourage different kinds of engagements (Pangrazio, 2018). Such scepticism creates a critical awareness of manipulative tactics like clickbait and misinformation (Henderson et al., 2020; Santos-Meneses, 2021). Scepticism is integral to how curatorial intentionality is mobilised because it shapes intentionality. In relation to gender justice, scepticism would be evident in young men's questioning of the gendered online content (e.g., how women are portrayed in online pornography) and architectures (e.g., how algorithms curate their online content in gendered ways) that shape their understandings of gender identities and relations.

In Chap. 2, leisure, work and identity, the young men demonstrated scepticism in their critique of the manipulative platform features within their online engagements, including algorithm-driven content and mechanisms that promote infinite scrolling. Such scepticism highlighted their recognition of how these technological structures foster addictive behaviours. However, as noted in the previous section, their attempts to moderate and regain control over their screen time were thwarted by these algorithms and mechanisms. Many of the young men, despite this recognition, found it difficult to be away from their devices and reported being stuck in patterns they knew to be harmful, unproductive and time consuming. The young men also expressed scepticism about the authenticity of the content they consumed. They were well aware of the performative nature of online self-presentation where content is curated differently for different audiences. Similar to their recognition of the performative nature of online anonymity, they questioned the authenticity of these presentations and the affordances within particular spaces that enabled them to express views they would not express in other online and offline spaces including views that are harmful to others. In relation to self-improvement content, the young men expressed scepticism towards influencers and their content (including Tate) as being fake, only about click bait and financial gain, as time-wasting and as bad role models for young men.

In Chap. 3, the young men's scepticism extended to online communities, where they recognised both the potential for connection and the risks of harm and abuse. As with their views about expressions of identity, the young men were sceptical about the authenticity of relationships and content within these communities particularly the mechanisms within gaming environments and platforms like X (formerly, Twitter) and Reddit that promote social polarisation, online hate and toxicity. They named social processes such as 'band wagoning', where enthusiastic individuals come together to express often negative and polarising views, and competitive male-dominated cultures, as enabled by these environments and platforms and as producing and amplifying toxicity and verbal abuse. Such scepticism is productive for gender justice in its potential to challenge and transform these gendered engagements.

In Chap. 4, scepticism was evident in the young men's concerns about being led astray and their concerns with misinformation. As already noted in relation to curatorial intentionality, the young men's critical awareness of the way algorithms work — to track and monitor their online engagements, lead them to harmful content, curate content to reinforce negative ideologies and behaviours, and affirm rather than broaden existing views—illustrates a strong scepticism about platform architectures designed to increase online engagement. Also noted earlier, such scepticism included a recognition of the influence of algorithms in directing male-identified users towards masculinist content through feed curation and a questioning of the authenticity and online infrastructures that elevate such content. In discussions of sex, intimacy, and privacy (Chap. 5), the young men's questioning of the assumptions and biases within the content of online pornography, including the platform affordances and algorithms that encourage them to engage in these spaces, illustrates their scepticism. The young men question the assumptions about them as young men that produce the algorithms that generate pornography in their social media feeds—i.e., assumptions that they would welcome the infiltration of pornography in their feeds (this is a particular kind of pornography that portrays women as sexual objects and men as sexually entitled). Such scepticism reflects hope for gender justice because it challenges the dominant tropes about young men and pornography that are embedded in these masculinised and sexist algorithms. In the area of privacy and security, the young men's scepticism was evident in their critical awareness of the manipulative tactics and misinformation produced within the context of scams, catfishing, and identity fraud, particularly in relation to older family members' vulnerability to online exploitation.

Ethical Engagement and Gender Justice

Ethical engagement is conceptualised in this book as a process of ongoing action and transformation in relation to what an individual understands to be important and good for themselves and others (Jenkins in Keddie et al., 2021). It is about accepting responsibility and accountable for one's actions and how they impact others (Keddie et al., 2021). Ethical engagement shapes how curatorial intentionality and scepticism are enacted. In relation to gender justice, ethical engagement would be evident in young men's awareness and acceptance of responsibility for how actions such as non-consensual sexting may harm others.

Across all of the chapters, our analysis highlighted the young men's struggles with ethical online engagement. In Chap. 2, leisure, work and identity, the young men reported their struggles with 'self-control' in terms of managing their excessive use of social media, and with authentic self-expression in digital spaces. They attempted to reconcile these struggles to be more in line with their desire for more meaningful and healthier online and offline engagements and experiences through disengaging and deleting apps. Further struggles for ethical engagement were evident in the young men's approach to influencers—to the extent that they sought out content that they understood as important and good for them—whether that was about an ethics of self-discipline and self-sufficiency or other forms of male empowerment. Sometimes these struggles extended to considering how their actions impacted on others. For example, the young men's critique of the narrow version of masculinity promoted by some influencers (who lack emotional sensitivity) was mobilised in ethical ways towards gender justice. That is, there was a questioning of the gendered online content that reproduces sexism and misogyny and a consideration of the risks and harms associated with anonymity, including how it enables harassment and unethical behaviours.

In Chap. 3, connection, community and conflict, similar ethical struggles were identified in the young men's attempts to curate their online engagements in ways that minimised negativity. A desire for a more ethical engagement online was evident in the young men's critique of the lack of accountability within online gaming environments for addressing hostility and abuse, the emotional toll of online hostility, exposure to negativity and harassment, the impacts of toxic interactions on their mental health, and their efforts to disengage from these spaces. In Chap. 4, the young men's ethical struggles were apparent in their desire to mitigate the power of algorithms to lead them astray (through disengaging or selecting 'not interested') and in their efforts to address misinformation (in their caution about accepting the validity, biases and truth of online content). However, this desire for ethics, while extending to a concern for others (who are unable to detect and resist misinformation), did not extend to considering the gendered dimensions of misinformation (especially in relation to Tate) in terms of its impacts on girls and women.

In Chap. 5, the young men expressed ethical struggles with online pornography. Such struggles were apparent in their efforts to navigate the ubiquity of pornography in their online lives, the 'battles' they experienced with addiction including the shame and regret they felt about this addiction, and the ways in which pornography distorted their ideas of sexual consent and their relationships with intimate partners and girls/women. Interspersed with these struggles was a concern about the impact of online pornography on younger generations. In such struggles, the young men were attempting to mitigate what they viewed as unethical in relation to online pornography. In this chapter, we also foregrounded the young men's ethical navigation of intimate image sharing. For these young men, trust and caution were central to ethical online intimacy and in this sense, many were highly aware of how actions such as non-consensual sexting harm others. These moves are productive for supporting gender justice (e.g., supporting trusting and mutually respectful gender relations). Further ethical struggles in this chapter were evident in the young men's concerns about the compromising of privacy and safety online (relating to online scams, identity theft and the misuse of personal information) and their concerns that regulation and censorship may undermine free speech.

These ethical struggles across all of the chapters tended to be framed at a personal level where the focus was on what the young men felt was good and important for them, whether that be abstaining from posting, engaging with Andrew Tate, declining trash talk in gaming environments, disrupting harmful algorithms, identifying misinformation or managing pornography addiction. While this individualised focus is ethical in involving the young men accepting responsibility and accountability for their actions, the young men only rarely considered how such engagements may impact on others. They also only rarely offered critique of broader considerations relating, for example, to the vital rôle that technology companies play in supporting ethical online engagements.

Reflexivity and Gender Justice

As noted in Chap. 1, reflexivity is an ongoing process of questioning and challenging issues of personal positionality. It is about adopting a self-critical stance in examining how our biases and prejudices (about gender, sexuality, race, class and ability) shape who and how we are (Keddie et al., 2021). Reflexivity informs the other dimensions in so far as it entails reflecting on how personal positionality shapes curatorial intentionality, scepticism and ethical engagement. In relation to gender justice, reflexivity involves critical consideration of how personal experiences with gender influence interpretations of digital content (e.g., awareness that young men's greater consumption and acceptance of pornography in comparison to young women's concerns about pornography (Martellozzo et al., 2016) relates to gendered positionality and men's greater tendencies to accept the dominant tropes of pornography).

Across all of the chapters, there was evidence of reflexivity to the extent that the young men considered and sometimes questioned how their positional biases shaped their online engagements. However, this reflexivity rarely extended to a self-critical stance about how biases and prejudices about gender, sexuality, race, class and ability may shape this engagement. In Chap. 2, leisure, work and identity, for example, a level of reflexivity was evident in how the young men contemplated their sense of authenticity and self-expression in digital spaces and their tendency to be more genuine with close friends and family in private digital spaces compared to broader social circles. In this chapter, a level of reflexivity and self-critique was apparent in the young men's engagements with influencer content. Their questioning of the gendered online content that reproduces sexism and misogyny implied an awareness of how gender positioning shapes interpretations of digital content. In some ways, this questioning reflected a self-critical stance in relation to biases about gender. Further reflexivity in this chapter can be detected in the agency exercised by the young men in how they presented themselves online. Their reluctance to post and their self-consciousness around what they posted, for example, was shaped by broader discourses of masculinity as stoic, competitive and invulnerable. In this regard, the young men can be seen as adopting a critical stance in identifying the biases about gender that shape their behaviours. While they navigate these discourses by choosing not to post, thus reinforcing them, there is a recognition that they are constrained by gendered pressures to curate themselves to conform to unrealistic masculine body standards and to compete with others in relation to these and other life standards.

In Chap. 3, reflexivity is apparent in how the young men align their desire for connection and belonging with improving their emotional and social well-being. This reflexivity, as noted in the previous paragraph, to some extent indicates a questioning and challenging of traditional masculinity as stoic, competitive and invulnerable. In relation to the gaming environments discussed in this chapter, a reflexive and self-critical stance in relation to how the biases of gender shape online engagement is evident but limited. Some of the young men recognise that as male-dominated spaces, gaming reproduces gender, racial and ability biases expressed through trash talk and other online abuses. However, such toxicity tends to be normalised as part of competitive male spaces, with some of the young men viewing trash talk and aggression as an expected component of the gaming experience.

In Chap. 4 the young men's reflexivity is evident in their views about misinformation associated with representations of Andrew Tate. Many of the young men defend Tate as standing up for men in an environment where feminism is taking over and as providing helpful advice about male empowerment at a time when they are feeling powerless and censored. Such views are clearly reflexive in their critical consideration of how the young men's personal experiences with gender influence their interpretation of digital content. However, as noted in this chapter, this reflexivity does not align with gender justice because it fails to recognise and challenge the gendered dimensions of misinformation proffered by Tate especially relating to his sexism and misogyny and its impacts on girls and women.

In Chap. 5, sex, intimacy and privacy, reflexivity plays out in the young men's critical consideration of how their personal experiences of gender influence their interpretation of online pornography. The young men's awareness of the negative impacts of pornography on their own and others' lives suggests a self-critical stance about the gender biases in pornography that shape their engagement as young men (e.g., algorithms that feed them sexualised content to maximise their engagement) and impact on others (e.g., their critique of pornography's objectification of women and girls). The young men's critical consideration of their own negative experiences of pornography are such that they express concern about how these experiences will negatively impact on younger generations. Further reflexivity involving a self-critical stance about the personal gender biases shaping interpretation of digital content is evident in the young men's views about image-based abuse. Some recognise that women, on the basis of their gender, face harsher scrutiny, reputational harm and greater risks when their images are leaked, while men experience comparatively minimal social backlash. The young men's critical awareness of the gendered dimensions of sharing intimate content highlights a process of reflexivity—a questioning and challenging of the biases about gender that shape engagement. There is an implicit critique here of the inequitable power imbalances in the digital sex economy.

Cultivating Critical Digital Dispositions Towards Gender Justice

Many of these findings are heartening. They indicate young men's sophisticated capacities for navigating the complexities and contentions of their online worlds. They highlight an expert mobilising of the critical digital dispositions of curatorial intentionality, scepticism, ethical engagement and reflexivity. Some of these dispositions, as we have highlighted, are highly generative in supporting gender justice, but some are not. Given these findings, in this section of the chapter, we consider how educators and facilitators working with young men might enhance their digital agency and criticality to further cultivate dispositions towards gender justice. We offer a series of activity ideas designed to cultivate these dispositions. These activities, consistent with key research in this space (see Setty et al., 2024), recognise and centre young people's agency in negotiating and transforming digitally mediated norms about gender and masculinity (for a comprehensive education resource designed to support young men to tackle and prevent gendered harms in online and offline communities, see O'Rourke and Haslop, 2023).

Before we present the activities, it is important to consider the general conditions that are requisite to enabling this sort of gender justice work with young men—that relate to creating safe, respectful and trusting environments. The Australian eSafety Commission's report: *Supporting young men online: understanding young men's needs, the pull of harmful content and a way forward* (2025, p. 32) outlines some important principles:

- Strengths-Based Approach—Focus on celebrating what young men do well rather than centring discussions solely on their problematic behaviours. Recognising their capacity for empathy, curiosity, and critical thinking can provide a foundation for constructive engagement.
- Call Young Men In, Not Out—Rather than adopting a punitive approach, educators and facilitators are encouraged to engage young men in reflective conversations that invite dialogue and mutual understanding. This 'calling in' method fosters collaboration rather than alienation.
- Intersectional Approach—Recognise that young men are not a homogenous group. Educators and facilitators should consider the intersecting influences of race, class, sexuality, and ability when developing interventions or educational programs.
- Tailored Communication—Effective engagement requires using language that resonates with young men while remaining accessible and relevant to the communities they belong to.
- Avoid Alarmist Narratives—Fear-based messaging about online harms can be counterproductive. Instead, provide nuanced discussions that acknowledge both the challenges and benefits of digital engagement in fostering more productive conversations.
- Building Emotional Literacy—Encouraging young men to develop emotional intelligence can help them navigate online and offline relationships in healthier ways.
- Practical Tools and Skills—Providing young men with tangible strategies for critical engagement with digital content, self-regulation, and ethical online participation equips them to navigate digital spaces more effectively.
- Peer-Led Approaches—Initiatives that involve young men learning from and supporting each other tend to be more impactful, as peer influence is a powerful factor in shaping attitudes and behaviours.

- Face-to-Face Engagement—While digital interventions are important, in-person discussions remain a crucial element of effective engagement, allowing for deeper reflection and relational connection.

These principles are important in setting up a context conducive to critically exploring issues of gender justice with boys and young men. Such work is inherently difficult and discomforting given that it involves addressing the practices of masculine entitlement that lead to gender injustice (Keddie, 2021). Discussions about gender justice can be emotionally intense—shame, resistance or defensiveness can obstruct or enable critical engagement. Educators and facilitators must recognise and support boys and young men to feel and articulate (rather than avoid) these strong emotions. Creating safe, respectful and trusting environments is key to supporting this process it is also key in helping boys and young men to recognise, understand and transform the practices of complicity that reproduce inequitable gender relations (Keddie, 2021).

The following presents a series of activity ideas drawn from the findings and analysis presented in this book that may be helpful in fostering young men's critical digital dispositions for gender justice through curatorial intentionality, scepticism, ethical engagement and reflexivity. As already noted, such activities will be most generative in an environment where young men feel safe, included and respected. They will also be most generative in contexts where educators and facilitators are engaging in their own critically reflexive work around their gender (and other) biases, their views about what constitutes gender justice and how this shapes their relationships and pedagogies with students (Keddie et al., 2021). Ideally, they will have developed close and trusting relationships with the boys and young men they are working with (see Keddie & Mills, 2007; Keddie & Bartel, 2021). Important here is connecting with where young men are at in their gender justice knowledges, supporting them to broaden their understandings of gender, power, masculinity and inequity, facilitating their recognition and critique of gender harms (including their own complicity in reproducing these harms) and fostering actions or activism towards gender justice (Keddie & Mills, 2007; Keddie & Bartel, 2021). Requisite to the effectiveness of the activity ideas that follow are these conditions and knowledges.

The AI tool Chat GPT was used to support the production of these activity ideas. Drawing on the previous text sections—(1) curatorial intentionality and gender justice, (2) scepticism and gender justice, (3) ethical engagement and gender justice, and (4) reflexivity and gender justice — Chat GPT was asked to create a series of activities to support young men's critical digital literacies for gender justice. The activities produced were modified and edited for clarity and relevance.

Activity Ideas to Cultivate Critical Digital Dispositions for Gender Justice

Curatorial Intentionality for Gender Justice

Hack Your Feed
This activity is designed to develop awareness of algorithmic curation and support participants to diversify their digital consumption. Over one week, participants will track and document their social media engagement, noting the type of content they like, share, and comment on. They will identify patterns in their recommendations and reflect on potential biases, such as predominantly male content or reinforcement of gender stereotypes. Participants will then experiment with intentional digital behaviour by following new creators, engaging with gender-just content, and observing changes in their recommendations. In a group discussion, they will analyse how algorithms shape gender perspectives and develop strategies to disrupt echo chambers.

Content Remix Challenge
This activity encourages participants to critically engage with digital media and create counter-narratives that challenge restrictive ideas about masculinity. In small groups, participants will identify a trending meme, video, or post that reinforces harmful gender norms. They will then create an alternative version that promotes gender inclusivity and justice using digital tools such as TikTok, Instagram Reels, or Canva. Once the content is complete, the group will discuss its potential impact, considering audience reactions and challenges in spreading gender justice messages online. The discussion will focus on the ways digital content shapes perceptions of masculinity and the opportunities for using social media to shift these narratives.

Scepticism for Gender Justice

Behind the Clickbait
This activity is designed to develop participants' capacities to critically assess the gendered messages and persuasive techniques used by influencers. Participants will select a male influencer known for shaping discussions on masculinity, analysing his content for persuasive strategies such as emotional appeals, fear-mongering, or aspirational messaging. They will identify gendered themes and potential biases in the influencer's messaging, then develop strategies to engage critically with such content. The session will conclude with a discussion on what makes influencers' messages compelling, how to distinguish between informative and manipulative content, and how to challenge misleading narratives.

Algorithms Detective
This activity is designed to sharpen scepticism by focusing on the hidden architectures that govern digital engagement. Participants will create two or three new social media accounts, each with different user profiles (e.g., one aligned with male-dominant fitness or gaming content, another centred on stereotypically feminine interests, and another aligned with gender-equity/feminism). Over the course of a week, they will track and document the recommendations, advertisements, and trending content suggested to each account. In small groups, participants will compare how algorithms differently curate online experiences, paying attention to recurring patterns in gender representation, reinforcement of hyper- or traditional masculinity and femininity, or promotion of inclusive perspectives. A follow-up discussion will guide learners to critically examine the commercial logics, persuasive architectures, and platform affordances driving these differences. By acting as "algorithm detectives," participants move beyond critiquing content alone to interrogating the systemic forces that structure what appears in their feeds.

Ethical Engagement for Gender Justice

Be the Moderator
This activity encourages participants to critically engage with the responsibilities of content moderation in shaping online discourse. Participants take on the role of content moderators for an online platform and are

presented with a set of real or fictional posts, comments, and interactions that include both gender-just and harmful content. In small groups, they decide which content should be amplified, challenged, or de-platformed and justify their choices. The activity concludes with a discussion on ethics and the role of content moderation, collective responsibility, intervention strategies, and how digital cultures can be reshaped for greater gender equity.

The Ethics of Digital Trust
This activity explores the role of trust, privacy, and consent in digital interactions, particularly in intimate or social media-driven spaces. Participants will analyse case studies involving image-based abuse, non-consensual content sharing, and digital privacy breaches, discussing their implications and ethical considerations. They will work in groups to co-create a "Digital Trust Code" outlining key principles for ethical online engagement, ensuring that issues of consent and accountability are addressed. The session will conclude with a reflection on personal and collective responsibilities in maintaining digital trust and fostering a culture of digital accountability.

Reflexivity for Gender Justice

Who Shapes My Feed?
This activity encourages deep reflexivity by guiding participants to critically examine how their personal experiences, social identities, and biases shape their engagement with digital content. Participants will conduct a digital self-audit, tracking their media consumption over a week. As they analyse patterns, they will consider how their positionality, such as being young men, students, or members of certain social or cultural groups, influences their interpretations and preferences. In small groups, they will discuss how gendered experiences shape their digital habits and how social norms around masculinity influence the types of content they follow, such as self-improvement influencers, gaming culture, or hypermasculine fitness content. By engaging in self-critical dialogue, they will interrogate how gendered, racial, and class-based assumptions structure their engagement with digital platforms including how this engagement impacts on others

Redesigning the Game

This activity examines gender norms in gaming cultures and develops alternative principles for inclusive gaming communities. Participants will identify common gendered themes in gaming environments relating to competition, exclusion, and harassment. Drawing on a range of different games, participants will analyse the architectures, content and relations within these games that reinforce or challenge these norms. In small groups, they will design alternative gaming principles or community guidelines that promote inclusivity and ethical engagement. They will then present and discuss strategies for fostering more equitable gaming spaces, focusing on the challenges and opportunities of making gaming communities both competitive and respectful.

These activities are designed to foster critical digital dispositions for gender justice. By engaging with curatorial intentionality, scepticism, ethical engagement, and reflexivity, they focus on supporting young men to identify, challenge, and transform the content, relations and architectures that produce online gendered harms. Moving beyond traditional digital literacy, these activities integrate critical perspectives on gender and power towards equipping young men with the capacity to navigate digital environments more ethically. They are designed to support an active reshaping of online engagements in ways that promote more gender-inclusive online cultures.

Broader Responsibilities

The activity ideas in the previous section are useful starting points towards cultivating young men's critical digital dispositions for gender justice. It is well recognised that educators play an important role in this space and should be professionally supported to teach such activities especially given their focus on sensitive and contentious issues. Regarding school education, the Australian Curriculum provides general guidance for teachers to connect online safety education to other areas of the curriculum. More targeted guidance for addressing gender-based digital harms is offered through resources such as the *Building respectful relationships curriculum: stepping out against gender-based violence* (Ollis, 2024). This excellent resource builds on previous respectful relationships curricula to critically explore the links between media, gender and the sexualisation of bodies, power, consent and respectful relationships (Ollis, 2024). Addressing gender-based digital harms is, however, not just an educational imperative. Educative efforts to support young men's critical and gender-just engagements online must be supported by systemic changes at the policy level. Without broader regulatory and institutional interventions, individual and educational efforts for gender justice will be limited.

Policymakers and technology companies play a crucial role in supporting online gender justice. At the forefront of efforts to regulate online platforms to mitigate gender-based harms is the Australian eSafety Commission. The *Safety by Design Industry Guide* (eSafety Commissioner, 2024) draws attention to the growing risks of technology-facilitated gender-based violence (TFGBV). TFGBV includes sexual harassment, coercive control, stalking, image-based abuse and deepfake pornography, forms of abuse that disproportionately impact women and girls. To address TFGBV, the guide advocates for greater service provider responsibility, user empowerment, and transparency and accountability. Rather than burdening individuals with sole responsibility for safety online, the guide supports much greater responsibility for platforms to be proactive in their anticipation and mitigation of risks at the design stage to ensure that content filtering, algorithmic interventions and AI-driven moderation work to prevent TFGBV before it occurs (see also, eSafety Commission, 2024).

More broadly, the *Online Safety Act* 2021 provides strong and expansive protections for Australians including against cyber abuse, image-based abuse, the blocking of abhorrent violent content, and new codes to regulate restricted and illegal content that is seriously harmful (eSafety Commission, 2021). Such protections and guidance are essential in reporting and removing harmful content. However, enforcement remains a challenge, especially when platforms do not comply with regulatory expectations. Moreover, national efforts to hold tech companies to account are complicated by the international reach of digital platforms, highlighting the imperative of national and international collaboration in the regulation of online harms.

It is clear that tech companies must be held to higher standards of transparency and accountability in addressing gender-based harms. It is also clear that addressing these harms requires a multi-stakeholder approach where educators, policymakers and technology companies work together to develop inclusive and effective strategies. A truly generative multi-stakeholder approach will focus on fostering a culture of digital responsibility, encouraging proactive interventions that reshape online spaces into equitable, inclusive, and safe environments for all users.

Conclusion

This book has highlighted the importance of better understanding how young men navigate their online worlds amid growing concerns about digital gender-based harm, 'toxic' masculinities, revenge porn and regressive 'manfluencers'. While policymakers and media narratives often focus on the risks young men pose online, there is limited research capturing their own perspectives on their digital experiences, both harmful and positive. Drawing on the voices of 117 young men, this book has provided nuanced insights into how young men engage with online spaces to express their identities, connect with others, address conflict, critique algorithms and misinformation, and navigate their exposure to pornography and their concerns with privacy. It has explored the tensions they experience—between connection and harm, empowerment and manipulation—and highlighted the complexities of their digital lives beyond the prevailing view of young men as uncaring and uncritical about the digital content they consume, create and share. By foregrounding these nuances and tensions, the book has challenged narrow portrayals of young men's online lives and offered a more balanced approach to supporting their critical digital engagement.

The book has drawn attention to the significance of cultivating young men's critical digital dispositions for gender justice—these are dispositions that involve interrogating the digital cultures that promote rigid ideas and enactments of gender and masculinity towards creating more equitable and gender just digital spaces (Henry et al., 2021). They engage with young men's existing practices of critical digital literacy—their curatorial intentionality, their strong sense of scepticism, their desire for ethical engagement and their ongoing reflexivity—to focus on gender justice. The tensions and struggles experienced by the young men in this book reveal that many are already engaging with these gender justice dispositions, from their critique of the misogynist and sexist messages of Andrew Tate to their concerns with the distorted ideas of sexual consent in pornography. Others, however, are reproducing gender injustice through their embracing of influencer content and gaming cultures that promote rigid and harmful expressions of masculinity. The series of activity ideas drawn from the book's findings and analyses are presented as helpful starting points in directing young men's already highly developed practices of curatorial intentionality, scepticism, ethical engagement and reflexivity towards gender justice.

Cultivating these critical digital dispositions for gender justice necessitates broader systemic change. As this book highlights, despite their critical awareness of how platform architectures and algorithms shape their online engagement, the young men struggle to navigate these architectures and algorithms in ethical ways and they generally accept personal responsibility for how, what and who they engage with online. Moreover, the young men's digital agency is often thwarted by deeply embedded algorithmic logics that continue to curate content and interactions that are harmful. Given the unprecedented pace and changing affordances of digital technologies, it is clear that policymakers must continue to work with technology companies, educators and young men themselves to cultivate ethical, responsible, and inclusive participation. Existing regulatory frameworks offer critical steps in mitigating digital harms, yet their effectiveness depends on consistent enforcement and accountability from tech companies. Only through a multi-stakeholder effort can we create digital spaces that not only protect individuals from harm but also actively work toward transformative gender justice.

References

eSafety Commission. (2021). *The online safety act*. https://www.esafety.gov.au/newsroom/whats-on/online-safety-act

eSafety Commission. (2024). *Gendered violence*. https://www.esafety.gov.au/key-topics/gendered-violence

eSafety Commissioner. (2024). *Safety by design: Technology, gendered violence and safety by design*. https://www.esafety.gov.au/sites/default/files/2024-09/SafetyByDesign-technology-facilitated-gender-based-violence-industry-guide.pdf

eSafety Commissioner. (2025). *Supporting young men online: Understanding young men's needs, the pull of harmful content and the way forward*. https://www.esafety.gov.au/sites/default/files/2025-02/Supporting-young-men-online-report-2.pdf?v=1739413603931

Henderson M. J., Shade L. R., Mackinnon K. (2020). Every click you make: Algorithmic literacy and the digital lives of young adults. AoIR Selected Papers of Internet Research. https://doi.org/10.5210/spir.v2020i0.11233

Henry, N., Stefani, V., & Alice, W. (2021). Digital citizenship in a global society: A feminist approach. *Feminist Media Studies, 22*(8), 1972–1989.

Keddie, A. (2021). Engaging boys in gender transformative pedagogy: Navigating discomfort, vulnerability and empathy. *Pedagogy, Culture & Society, 30*(3), 401–414.

Keddie, A., & Bartel, D. (2021). The affective intensities of gender transformative work: An actionable framework for facilitators working with boys and young men. *Journal of Men and Masculinities, 24*(5), 740–759.

Keddie, A., Lees, D., & Delaney, M. (2021). Reflexivity, ethics and accountability: Facilitators working for gender transformation with boys and men. *Journal of Gender Studies, 32*(3), 259–269. https://doi.org/10.1080/09589236.2021.1990031

Keddie, A., & Mills, M. (2007). *Teaching boys: Developing classroom practices that work.* Routledge.

Martellozzo, E., Monaghan, A., Adler, J. R., Davidson, J., Leyva, R., & Horvath, M. A. (2016). I wasn't sure it was normal to watch it... A quantitative and qualitative examination of the impact of online pornography on the values, attitudes, beliefs and behaviours of children and young people. Middlesex University, NSPCC, OCC.

Ollis, D. (2024). *Building respectful relationships: Stepping out against gender-based violence.* Department of Education.

O'Rourke, F. and Haslop, C. (2023). #Men4change: Tackling and transforming harmful gendered norms and behaviours - a toolkit for youth leaders and activists, Liverpool, U.K: University of Liverpool.

Pangrazio, L. (2018). *Young people's literacies in the digital age: Continuities, conflicts and contradictions.* Routledge.

Santos-Meneses, L. F. (2021). Thinking critically through controversial issues on digital media: Dispositions and key criteria for content evaluation. *Thinking Skills and Creativity, 42*, 100927. https://doi.org/10.1016/j.tsc.2021.100927

Setty, E., Ringrose, J., & Hunt, J. (2024). From 'harmful sexual behaviour' to 'harmful sexual culture': Addressing school-related sexual and gender-based violence among young people in England through 'post-digital sexual citizenship'. *Gender and Education, 36*(5), 434–452.

Stenalt, M. H. (2021). Digital student agency: Approaching agency in digital contexts from a critical perspective. *Frontline Learning Research, 9*(3), 52–68. https://doi.org/10.14786/flr.v9i3.697

Weinstein, E. & James, C. (2022). Behind Their Screens: What Teens are Facing and Adults are Missing, Cambridge, The MIT Press.

Index

A. Keddie, M. Flood, *Young Men's Online Lives*,
https://doi.org/10.1007/978-3-031-99980-2

GPSR Compliance

The European Union's (EU) General Product Safety Regulation (GPSR) is a set of rules that requires consumer products to be safe and our obligations to ensure this.

If you have any concerns about our products, you can contact us on ProductSafety@springernature.com

In case Publisher is established outside the EU, the EU authorized representative is:

Springer Nature Customer Service Center GmbH
Europaplatz 3
69115 Heidelberg, Germany

Batch number: 08977887

Printed by Printforce, the Netherlands